Beyond the Rules
Writing with
Clarity, Power, and Style

by
Ruth Fennick
Elaine Dion
Mary Peters

illustrated by Vanessa Filkins

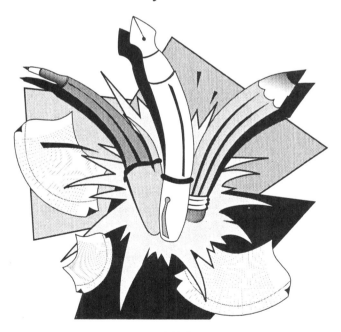

Publisher
Instructional Fair • TS Denison
Grand Rapids, Michigan 49544

The authors wish to thank the following for their assistance and their generosity.

Excerpt from *Imitate the Tiger* reprinted courtesy of Jan Cheripko and Boyds Mills Press.

Excerpt from "Open Shirts or Giant Shorts, It's All a Matter of Fitting In" reprinted courtesy of Tom Martin, the complete work originally printed in the *Hancock County Journal Pilot*, Carthage, Illinois.

Excerpt from "The Name Game Gets Wackier Every Year" reprinted courtesy of Tom Martin, the complete work originally published 12 January 1997 in the *Macomb Journal*, Macomb, Illinois.

ISBN: 1-56822-625-X
Beyond the Rules: Writing with Clarity, Power, and Style
Copyright © 1998 by Instructional Fair • TS Denison
2400 Turner Avenue NW
Grand Rapids, Michigan 49544

Table of Contents

Chapter One: Language Choices

Chapter Two: Writing for Different Audiences and Occasions

Chapter Three: Organizing Ideas

Chapter Four: Making Ideas Clear and Concise

Chapter Five: Creating Your Own Style

Chapter Six: Using Punctuation for Effect

About This Book

This book goes beyond grammatical terms and rules to examine the effect of stylistic choices. To many people style means personal preference, and to some degree personality is reflected in style. But style also has to do with ways of using language strategically. The words we select and the way we arrange them reflect choices that we make, consciously or unconsciously, every time we speak or write. The activities in this book are intended to help students become more conscious of these choices and of the effect they have on readers.

Although research articles suggest that study of traditional grammar has a limited effect on writing ability, teachers are reluctant to abandon this staple of the language arts curriculum, feeling intuitively that something important would be lost. This book suggests an alternative, applied approach to language study for students in the middle school and upper grades. Rather than supplanting traditional grammar, it emphasizes application and refinement of formal rules for use in real writing situations. Students are asked to use the terms and rules they learned in their study of formal grammar as the foundation for linguistic experimentation as they attempt to make their own writing more clear, more concise, more elegant, and, thus, more powerful.

Because this book emphasizes style rather than correct form, rarely will students be advised to follow particular rules. Instead, they will be offered general guidelines for making their writing clear and concise. They will be asked to look at the work of other writers to see how it succeeds or how it can be improved, and they will be encouraged to make similar improvements in their own writing.

In these activities students learn that writing is not a right and wrong exercise, but a complex medium that asks writers to make sophisticated judgments. Just as they must make choices about what words will best convey their intentions, they must also make choices about what structures—and even what mechanics and visual presentation—will help them to create the desired effect in the reader. In the process, they gain greater understanding of the reasons behind the rules; they see that writing effectively is more complex than simply producing a grammatically correct text; and they learn strategies that can be applied in all the writing they do.

This book is comprised of six chapters: "Language Choices," "Writing for Different Audiences and Occasions," "Organizing Ideas," "Making Ideas Clear and Concise," "Creating Your Own Style," and "Using Punctuation for Effect." Units within these chapters are divided into three sections: "Understanding Choices," "Recognizing Choices," and "Making Choices," introducing the concept to students, asking them to identify the linguistic structure or strategy in a written passage, and, finally, requiring them to demonstrate the strategy in their own writing.

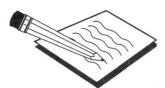

CHAPTER 1
Language Choices

Understanding Writers' Choices

Writing Effectively

Have you ever read a short story, article, poem, or novel and enjoyed it so much that you lost track of time or were disappointed that it had to end? If you have had this experience, then for some reason the author's words had a special appeal to you. They caused you to read on with enthusiasm and to enter the author's world.

1. Think about the various selections you have read. Write the title of a favorite work here. _____

2. List a few reasons why this selection is so memorable.

   _____

   _____

   _____

Share your selection in small groups. Discuss with group members what makes your selection so memorable. Are several titles repeated? Or is there a wide variety?

3. Try to locate the favorite work you listed above and examine it more closely. What makes the language so appealing to you?

   _____

   _____

Your group members possibly generated many different titles and gave many different reasons for selecting favorites. These reasons are based on personal taste or preference and are similar to our preferences for the clothes we wear and the ways we style our hair.

Writers' Styles

You have probably noticed that writers write differently. What you may not have noticed are the specifics that make their writing unique. Read the following passages and answer the questions that appear on the chart on the next page.

I never see it happen. When Geltson runs in to block the punt, I drop back to block on the return play. I'm shield-blocking Hudson's wide receiver, Tommy Jeklowski. Suddenly, Jeklowski grabs my face mask. He pulls me down, swings me around, twists my face mask, and rips my helmet off my head.

Jan Cheripko, *Imitate the Tiger*

The long hallway of blue lockers blurred as Nicole's eyes filled with tears. She started running toward the bathrooms at the end of the hall. She felt like she was in a nightmare running from the most horrible monsters imaginable. But everything was real—the lockers, the hall, the school, and the sick feeling inside her. Once Nicole had finally made it to the bathroom, she threw open the stall door and just stood there for a minute. She then pulled back her silky black hair, and very carefully stuck two fingers down her throat.

Sumer Allensworth, eighth-grade student

My name is Tom, but it could've been Sidney. I'm not sure exactly why, but my dad wanted to name me Sidney. He doesn't talk much about it now, but I'll bet there was some conversation before I was born. Mom won out though, and I'm glad for that. I like my name. It's simple, solid, traditional.

Tom Martin, newspaper columnist

Name _____

Compare each author's style by filling out the chart below. Do you see differences in the first words of each sentence? In the length of each sentence? In the verbs?

# of Sentence	First Word	# of Words in Sentence	Verb(s)
Passage One 1			
2			
3			
4			
5			
Passage Two 1			
2			
3			
4			
5			
6			
Passage Three 1			
2			
3			
4			
5			
6			

Examining Different Styles

Every published writer has his or her own style. Careful reading will help you become aware of the strategies various authors use to achieve their unique styles. Select one activity from numbers 1, 2, and 3 and one activity from numbers 4, 5, and 6. Complete them on another sheet of paper and then share your findings with the class.

1. In her short story "Charles," Shirley Jackson effectively uses -ly words with variations of the word *said*. Read Jackson's story and list the -ly/*said* choices. How do these choices affect the story?

2. O. Henry includes many similes in "The Ransom of Red Chief." Read O. Henry's story and list several of the similes. What do these choices add to the story?

3. Skim a few pages of *The Call of the Wild* by Jack London. Look at sentence length and word usage. Write down four words whose meaning you do not know.

4. Read "The Highwayman" by Alfred Noyes. Notice the poem's figurative language. Noyes includes similes, metaphors, personification, and even adds vivid colors. Try to find two examples of each of these figures of speech and two examples of colors. Try writing the poem as prose, leaving out all the figures of speech and all the colors. Discuss with a partner the differences between the original poem and your story.

5. Read two poems by Emily Dickinson. Note the length of each line and the rhythm of each line. Count the number of syllables each line contains. Place stress marks above each syllable that receives emphasis. Does Dickinson's style make her poems easy or difficult to read?

6. Choose three works you have read recently. Consider the following language choices that each author made.
   A. Did the writer use mostly long or short sentences?
   B. Did the writer use present or past tense verbs?
   C. Did the writer use slang or formal language?
   D. Did the writer use a lot of punctuation, for example, commas, semicolons, and dashes; or did the writer use very little punctuation?

Regardless of the above activities you chose to complete, you probably noticed that you read works of wonderful authors who have made different choices, both in message and style.

Recognizing What You Already Know

Language Conventions

The activities on the previous page show that good authors employ a wide variety of language and structure choices quite effectively. They also show that those same language and structure choices are available to you as a writer. However, many beginning writers feel uncertain about making choices, mainly because there are so very many of them to make—choices about content, language, sentences, paragraphs, and even punctuation.

To communicate clearly and concisely, you need to make appropriate choices for each writing occasion. And the more you know about language, the more likely you are to make good choices.

You already know a lot about the English language (probably more than you realize) and, consequently, already have many choices available. The next few activities are designed to refresh your memory and to renew your confidence in your knowledge of language.

Complete Sentences

For most occasions complete sentences produce the clearest text for your reader. Read the following groups of words. Place an X in front of those which are complete sentences.

_____ 1. John, Susan, and Amy.

_____ 2. Enjoyed the movie.

_____ 3. Jeremy kicked the winning field goal.

_____ 4. Sarah made.

_____ 5. The freshmen built the prize-winning float.

If you marked numbers 3 and 5 as complete sentences, you made the correct choice! You probably recognized those groupings as complete sentences because of both their messages and their structures.

Sentence Structure

Structure is the order we give to our thoughts. We learn to read by moving our eyes across the page from left to right; our brains process information in that same left-to-right sequence. Eventually, as we become proficient readers, we expect to see that same order. Position becomes extremely important, so important, in fact, that when we read a sentence that does not follow this left-to-right structure, we experience difficulty understanding the passage.

To see how quickly you can order the structure of a sentence from left to right, try this experiment. Place the following words in the boxes below so that they form a complete sentence.

wrote   Susan   letters   three

[ ]   [ ]   [ ]   [ ]

If you ordered the structure from left to right, you probably created the following sentence: *Susan wrote three letters.* We expect to read the naming word first followed by some action, or a "doing" word. We also expect to see the adjective *three* come before the noun it modifies, *letters.* See how much you already know about the structure of our language!

However, you know even more than that. Now add the following word to the sample sentence by drawing an arrow to where you think it belongs.

[once]

Did you place it at the beginning? If so, you are correct! Did you place it at the end, or did you place it just before the verb? If so, you were also correct! The word *once* makes sense in several places: *Once Susan wrote three letters. Susan wrote three letters once. Susan once wrote three letters.* Like many adverbs, it can move around in a sentence. You may also place prepositional phrases in various positions in the above sentence. Add the following prepositional phrase to the above sentence: *in one day.* Write your new sentence here.

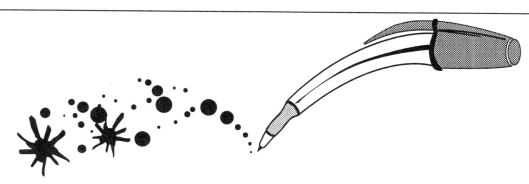

Types of Sentences

You know a lot about the structure of sentences. You also know a lot about the different types of sentences and when to use each type. You probably already use the following four types of sentences frequently in your own writing: declarative, interrogative, imperative, and exclamatory. A declarative sentence provides information. An interrogative sentence asks a question. An imperative sentence gives a command or makes a request. An exclamatory sentence shows strong feeling. Good writers use all four types of sentences effectively in their work.

Label each of the following sentences, DEC for declarative, INT for interrogative, IMP for imperative, and EXC for exclamatory. The answers appear on the next page.

_____ 1. Does Susan enjoy writing letters?

_____ 2. Mail those letters today, please.

_____ 3. How nice it is that you answered the letters so promptly!

_____ 4. Susan often writes letters for her grandmother, who has arthritis.

Punctuation

Although the structure and content of each sentence help the reader know when the sentence ends, punctuation also helps. The reader will naturally pause at a place where punctuation is needed. Punctuation then acts as signposts for your reader. To see what you know about punctuation, read the following paragraph and place punctuation marks where they are needed. The author's punctuation choices appear on the next page.

Mark Twain's *The Adventures of Tom Sawyer* contains many adventures the adventures truly begin when Huck and Tom go to the cemetery one night they stop walking just in time as they hear voices they then see Injun Joe, Muff Potter, and Dr. Robinson digging up a grave the boys watch in awe and see Injun Joe stab the doctor and blame the action on Muff who is drunk Tom and Huck swear never to tell a soul what they have witnessed

Nonstandard Forms

You not only know about sentences, but you also know about how and when the language works—and how and when it does not work. You probably already recognize many of the most obvious errors, like "ain't" and "knowed." These are misuses of the language, called *nonstandard forms.*

See whether you can find the nonstandard forms in the following sentences. First, fold the bottom part of this page on the dotted line so that you cannot see it. Then circle the word or words in each sentence that you would never use this way.

1. Christine learn how to play the piano by the time she was nine.

2. Annie, John, Mary, and Ernie enjoyed her vacation.

3. Carla read three book during vacation.

4. Mitchell gots too much homework this weekend.

5. Melissa and Michael have went to the grocery store.

----

1. Circle *learn* to apply the basic rule of past tense.
2. Circle *her* to show a mistake in agreement in number. Annie, John, Mary, and Ernie all went on the vacation, making it *their* vacation.
3. *Book* should be circled. Since Carla read three, the basic rule of adding -*s* to make many nouns plural applies.
4. Circle *gots,* which is nonstandard usage for *has.*
5. Circle *have went* because the principal part (past participle) is *have gone.*

These rules are what we accept as standard forms in our language. Not to follow them as speakers and writers would mark our work as being nonstandard. They are generally accepted by everyone and can be considered RULES.

*Answers, page 7: Types of Sentences: 1. INT, 2. IMP, 3. EXC, 4. DEC
Punctuation: Mark Twain's *The Adventures of Tom Sawyer* contains many adventures. The adventures truly begin when Huck and Tom go to the cemetery one night. They stop walking just in time as they hear voices. They then see Injun Joe, Muff Potter, and Dr. Robinson digging up a grave. The boys watch in awe and see Injun Joe stab the doctor and blame the action on Muff who is drunk. Tom and Huck swear never to tell a soul what they have witnessed.

Making Choices as Writers

Examining Your Own Style

Style in writing is a lot like style in other parts of your life. Although it requires you to follow some accepted conventions, it also allows for unique personal touches. For example, some people wear bright, bold colors and plaids and stripes. Others wear darker or softer colors and stick to tweeds or plain fabrics. In the same way, some writers use bold, dramatic adjectives and emphatic punctuation. Others use more subdued language and traditional punctuation.

1. Before looking at some of your own writing, see if you can identify the writers of the following passages. They are A) an eighth-grade student and B) a newspaper columnist. Place the letter in the blank to designate each author.

_____ With our great luck, the last steer decided it wanted to be back in its pen, so it jumped out of the pasture and ran back to the cattle barn. The next morning it was sitting next to the gate it had broken, wanting to get back into the pen with the other cattle. Go figure!

_____ Wearing T-shirts under a button-up shirt was the way men dressed for years. My dad still believes in the sheathing qualities of a plain, white, cotton T-shirt. He also believed his son should be protected. That didn't pose a problem until I entered junior high.

If you correctly identified the writer of each passage (the answers appear at the bottom of the next page), your speculation about each author's style was correct. You may have based your choices partly upon what you think each author would write and partly upon intuition. If you had read many more works written by these two writers, you would probably get a much better sense of their individual styles. As you write, you too will develop a style which is particular to you. You may have already made certain choices that identify your work. See whether your classmates can identify your writing style.

2. Write an original story, but do not put your name anywhere on the paper. Your teacher will collect your stories and redistribute them. Your job is to read each story and try to determine its author. Continue to pass the stories around the room until you have read everyone's story. Did you correctly guess the authors of many stories? Was your style recognized by your classmates?

Imitating Style

One way to learn about style is to imitate the choices that great writers have made. Their choices of words, sentence structure, and punctuation provide an excellent beginning place for work with style.

1. For instance, examine the first sentence of Edgar Allan Poe's "The Tell-Tale Heart": "True!—nervous—very dreadfully nervous I had been and am; but why *will* you say that I am mad?" First, begin by filling in the blanks with your own words.

True!—_____—very dreadfully _____ I had been and am; but why *will* you say that I am _____?

One student completed the above sentence in this way: "True!—shy—very dreadfully shy I had been and am, but why will you say that I am backward?" Notice Poe's use of the dash, exclamation point, and question mark as well as the structure of the sentence.

2. Now try to imitate the entire sentence below, substituting as many words and phrases as you wish. Be certain to retain the original structure of this sentence which appears later in "The Tell-Tale Heart": "Presently I heard a slight groan, and I knew it was the groan of mortal terror."

_____

_____   _____

One student wrote this sentence: "Presently I saw Raymond's beady eyes, and I knew they were the eyes of pure hatred." Imitating the style of published writers requires much time and effort, but the rewards are worth it. Imagine the effect of the above sentence about Raymond's eyes in a short story as compared with a sentence which merely states that his eyes are small or beady.

3. Find five sentences from your own reading that you find especially appealing or effective. Copy them on another sheet of paper. Then write a sentence imitating each sentence that you copied. Be certain to imitate the punctuation as well as the style. In fact, if you read "The Tell-Tale Heart" in its entirety, you will find that Poe utilizes the dash quite often (and quite effectively) throughout his story.

*Answers to page 9: First passage: A, Second passage: B

Experimenting with Style

Along with sentence structure and punctuation, word choice requires careful consideration. Think of the different words that you could use for *money: moola, cash, bread, dough,* and *currency* just begin the list—not to mention words for particular denominations like *two-bits, buck,* and *C-note.* Depending upon the author's audience and purpose, one may be chosen for a particular audience and another chosen for a different audience.

1. Imagine that you are writing a story about gangsters. Which term would you use to designate money in your story? _____

2. Now imagine that you are writing a letter to the president of the local bank. Which term would you use to refer to *money* in your letter? _____

3. In the first column of blanks, list three words that can be used in place of *slacks.* In the second column, list a writing situation in which it would be appropriate to use the word.

   _____   _____

   _____   _____

   _____   _____

4. Read the following passage. Fill in the blanks by circling the word in each column that you think the writer used.

Naming a kid Sigmund is not going to make him a(n) __A__. It will probably cause him some trouble on/in the __B__, though. By the same __C__, naming a kid Buck isn't going to turn him into a(n) __D__ bronco rider.

A	B	C	D
egg-head	playground	way	award-winning
intellectual	gymnasium	manner	vicious
brain	park	rule	tough-as-nails
genius	classroom	token	fiery

Creating a Comfortable Style

Select a passage or story that you have written or write a new one. Try three of the following activities.

1. Rewrite the passage using all short, declarative sentences.

2. Rewrite the passage using at least three interrogative sentences.

3. Rewrite the passage combining as many sentences as possible, making them either compound or complex sentences.

4. Change the tense of the passage. If you wrote the original in present tense, change it to past tense; if you wrote the original in past tense, change it to present tense.

5. Include many exclamatory sentences.

6. Write a passage using all action verbs (do not use *am, are, is, was,* or *were*).

Which passage do you like best? _____

Why? _____

_____

*Answers, Page 11: 4. A. intellectual, B. playground, C. token, D. tough-as-nails

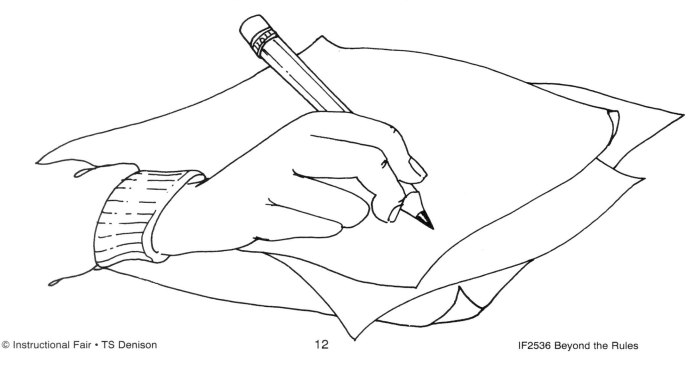

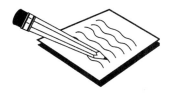

CHAPTER 2
Writing for Different Audiences and Occasions

Using First, Second, or Third Person

Understanding Choices

Using Pronouns

As a writer, one of the first things you will need to decide is your role in the particular writing situation. Sometimes you will want to turn the attention on yourself, sometimes on the reader, and sometimes on neither. The choice is yours. Using appropriate personal pronouns will make your writing more effective. Personal pronouns not only take the place of nouns (thereby avoiding repetition), but they also clarify your role as the writer. Personal pronouns are grouped according to who is speaking:

Person	Pronouns
first (person speaking)	I, me, we, us, my, mine, our, ours
second (person spoken to)	you, your, yours
third (person spoken about)	he, she, it, they, him, her, his, hers, its, their, theirs

Read the following sentences. Label each personal pronoun by placing a "1" above each first-person pronoun, a "2" above each second-person pronoun, and a "3" above each third-person pronoun.

Thank you for your prompt response to my letter of inquiry. The information in

your brochure makes your company sound quite interesting and innovative. I

would like to make my proofreading services available to you. I am enclosing a list

of references. They can be contacted at your convenience.

Would you say that the message focuses more on the person speaking, the person spoken to, or the person spoken about?

Recognizing Choices

Your choice of first-, second-, or third-person pronouns depends not only upon your role in the writing situation, but also upon your audience and your purpose for writing.

Personal Expression

Much of the writing you do involves personal expression. Personal expression is found in journal writing, personal notes (such as thank-you notes), and friendly letters. Because you will focus on your own thoughts and feelings, you will probably use many first-person pronouns, but you may also use some second-person pronouns. Second-person pronouns are especially useful in thank-you notes and messages of congratulations.

Fill in appropriate first-person pronouns in the following short paragraph from a friendly letter.

_____ really enjoyed going to the movie with Sarah last weekend. _____ saw a real thriller. At one point _____ was so nervous that I covered _____ eyes. Sarah had to nudge _____ so that I'd open them and see the ending.

Business Correspondence

When writing for business purposes, you will need to focus on the reader, even though you are involved in the interaction. For instance, if you are writing a letter inquiring about the possibility of a summer job, you are interested in it for yourself—but you should remember to focus on the reader. Focus on why your prospective employer would be interested in YOU.

Fill in the appropriate second-person pronouns in the following paragraph.

I recently read in the *Daily Times* that _____ firm is looking for lawn care workers. I would like to apply for this position. Because of my experience, I feel that I can be a great service to _____ company. Benefits to _____ would be prompt, dependable service and a neatly manicured entrance—thereby presenting _____ new and existing clients with a good initial impression.

*Answers, page 13: First person: my, I, my, I; Second person: you, your, your, your, you, your; Third person: They

Academic Writing

Although first-person pronouns are acceptable in some academic writing (such as a persuasive essay), in most academic writing, you will rarely use them. Because you will be focusing on the subject in academic writing, you will need to use third-person pronouns. For example, in research writing, it is the findings that are important. In academic writing, you will most likely focus on your subject.

Fill in the appropriate third-person pronouns in the following paragraph.

The survey was conducted by two seventh-grade students. John tabulated

_____ results in a pie graph, and Sarah used a bar graph to show _____

results. _____ collaborated to write a report which included the research

question, research methods, an explanation of _____ findings, and

_____ conclusions.

Creative Writing

Creative writing gives you the opportunity to choose which of the pronouns you will use—first-, second-, or third-person. Your choice will depend partly on whom you choose as a narrator. The narrator may be you, the writer, speaking through one of the characters in the story. If you create a narrator outside the story, you will use the character's name and third-person pronouns.

Fill in the pronouns in the following excerpt from *Anne of Green Gables*, which uses a third-person narrator.

Gilbert was head of the spelling class; now Anne, with a toss of _____ long,

red braids, spelled _____ down. One morning Gilbert had all _____

sums done correctly and had _____ name written on the blackboard on the

roll of honor; the next morning, Anne, having wrestled wildly with decimals the

entire evening before, would be first. One awful day _____ were tied and

_____ names were written up together.

Making Choices

Below are several writing situations. In the box at the right tell whether you think each would use primarily first-person, second-person, or third-person pronouns.

Audience	Document and Purpose	Writer	Person
third graders	a brochure providing information showing that regular brushing is necessary to healthy gums and teeth	school nurse	
president of local bank	a note thanking her for her donation of three computers to your language arts classroom	teacher	
readers of daily newspaper	an article in a newspaper showing results of a survey of homeowners' needs for goods and services	mayor	
yourself	journal entry recording your thoughts about your goals for the next two years	middle-school student	
first graders	fairy tale about a boy who is granted three wishes	high-school student	

Select one of the above and complete the writing assignment, choosing appropriate pronouns.

*Answers, page 15, second paragraph: her, him, his, his, they, their

Using Past, Present, or Future Tense

Understanding Choices

How do I know which verb tense to use?

As a rule, it is best to stick to a single tense throughout a report, essay, or story. Of course, even when a writer sticks to one tense, there may be places where the writer needs to change tense for a moment in order to express the meaning clearly. For example, in the following passage from an essay that is written primarily in present tense, the writer must occasionally change to past and future tenses to express the intended meaning.

> The American bald eagle *is* an endangered species. A hundred years ago, bald eagles *were* commonplace throughout the mountainous regions of the United States, but today very few of them still *exist*. Without programs to protect this endangered species, it *will disappear* within the next hundred years. This important American symbol *needs* our protection today.

Most of the time, you write in past tense about past events, in present tense about current events, and in future tense about things to come. However, there are exceptions to this rule. One important exception is the plot summary. A summary of a short story, a novel, a play, or a movie is usually written in present tense even though the action may be in the past or in the future. If you look at book covers, video jackets, and newspaper and magazine reviews, you will see that the standard practice among professional review writers is to use present tense for describing the plot of a story. The same is true for brochures on coming attractions distributed at movie theaters and video rental stores and in the movie sections of most television guide magazines.

To see this use of present tense in professional writing, find examples of plot summaries in several of the above media and supply the information requested below on two examples.

Media Type	Title	Plot Summary Excerpt	Present Tense Verbs

Recognizing Choices

Past or Present?

If you were writing a short story about fictional characters, what do you think would be the most logical tense to use to narrate their adventures? _____

Read the following excerpt from a children's story and notice the verbs as you read.

Freddie dashed across the open meadow, her heart pounding the whole way. There was no time to listen for gunshots. Her only hope against the hunters' bullets was the speed nature had given her. As she neared the burrow, Freddie stretched her furry little body into a full-length, head-first dive. Like a runner desperate to make home plate, Freddie flew through the air and then through the powder, taking a good three feet of snow with her as she slid down the hole and into the burrow. Her mother's scolding voice had never sounded so good.

Circle the verbs in the above passage. In what tense is this passage written? _____

Rewrite part of the above excerpt in the space below, replacing the verbs with a different tense. Then reread the passage to see whether the new verb tense improves or weakens the storytelling.

_____

_____

_____

_____

_____

_____

What verb tense do you prefer for the above narrative? _____

Why? _____

Past or Present?

If you were writing a plot summary for a book jacket, what tense do you think would be best? (Consider professional writers' standard practice.) _____

Read the following review of a famous adventure novel about a dog. Notice the verb tense used.

The Call of the Wild by Jack London is the dramatic story of the dog Buck. As the story begins, Buck is stolen from the family who loves him and has raised him from a pup. His new master, a sled driver who overworks and underfeeds his dogs, takes Buck on a long journey. Buck learns a lot about evil in the world from humans and other dogs. He learns not to trust everyone, and he learns how to fight for his life among a pack of abused and savage dogs. However, *The Call of the Wild* is also a story of love and devotion. Once Buck is rescued by a man who recognizes Buck's true nature, the man and the dog become friends for life. London's narrative of their exploits amid the hardships of the Yukon is one of the greatest adventure stories ever written.

Circle the verbs in the above passage. In what tense is this passage written? _____

Rewrite part of the above summary, replacing the verbs with a different tense. Then reread the passage and see whether the new tense improves or weakens the effect of the plot summary.

_____

_____

_____

_____

_____

_____

What verb tense do you think is best for the above review? _____

Why? _____

Past or Present?

If you were writing a letter to the principal of your school to explain a current problem in the school cafeteria, what tense would you use in your letter? _____

Read the following excerpt from such a letter and notice the verb tense that is used.

October 10, _____

Dear Mr. Johnson:

I am writing on behalf of the sixth-grade class to inform you of a problem in our school cafeteria. Our class has the last lunch period of the day. Lately it seems that almost every day at 12:40 p.m., when our class goes to lunch, the main lunch items are gone. Sometimes there are no cheeseburgers or pizza left, so we have to eat peanut butter or ham sandwiches instead.

Circle the verbs in the above passage. In what tense is this letter written? _____
Rewrite part of the above excerpt, replacing the verbs with a different verb tense. Reread the passage and see whether the new verb tense improves or weakens the letter.

October 10, _____

Dear Mr. Johnson:

_____

_____

_____

_____

_____

What verb tense do you think is best for the above letter? _____

Why? _____

Past or Present?

If you were writing a biographical report on a person born in 1564, what do you think would be the most logical tense to use in describing that person's life? _____

Read the following excerpt from a biographical essay. Notice the verbs used in this essay.

There are not many official records providing information about the life of William Shakespeare, the greatest dramatist of all times. From the information that is available, historians have concluded that Shakespeare was born in 1564 in Stratford-upon-Avon in England. He attended school in Stratford and probably worked for awhile in his father's shop. In 1582 he married Anne Hathaway, who was also from Stratford. For several years he was a schoolteacher in Stratford, but in 1588 he went to London to become an actor and a playwright.

Circle the verbs in the above passage. In what tense is this passage written? _____

Write a paragraph below about someone you admire. Your subject may be a friend or family member, a famous person who is living now, or someone who lived in the past.

_____

_____

_____

_____

_____

_____

_____

_____

What verb tense did you use primarily? _____

Why? _____

Making Choices

Personal Biography: You are writing a chapter in your own biography about a memorable time in your life (perhaps your most embarrassing moment). What tense will you use? _____

Why? _____

Video Promotion: You are a writer for a video company and you are writing a plot summary for the video jacket of a popular movie. What tense will you use? _____

Why? _____

Book Review: You are a writer for a bookstore. Your assignment is to write a review for the back cover of a favorite novel for young people. What tense will you use? _____

Why? _____

Prediction: You are a writer for a magazine called *Future Lifestyles*. You are writing an article that predicts an average teenager's day in the year 2050. What tense will you use?_____

Why? _____

Short Story: You write children's books for a living. You are writing a fairy tale for children. What tense will you use? _____

Why? _____

Letter: You are writing to a friend who lives far away and does not know what is going on in your life. You explain what movies, books, and music you are interested in, who your friends are, what is happening in your town, and what classes you are taking. What tense will you use?_____

Why? _____

Diary: You are somewhere in an exciting situation (watching a tornado from a car in a ditch, observing take-off in the cockpit of a DC-10, lifting off from Cape Canaveral in a space shuttle, or riding an elephant on a Safari in Nairobi). You are recording the events on a tape recorder so you can write them with all the drama and excitement of the real moment. You want the reader to feel "You are there!" What tense will you use? _____

Why? _____

Using Active or Passive Voice

Understanding Choices

The term *voice* is used to describe who or what is performing the action. When you read the following sentences, you will notice that they have almost the same words and basically the same meaning.

    A. John published research about diabetes.
    B. Research on diabetes was published by John.
    C. The research on diabetes was published.

1. What is the subject in sentence A? _____

2. What is the verb in sentence A? _____

3. What is the subject in sentence B? _____

4. What is the verb in sentence B? _____

5. What is the subject in sentence C? _____

6. What is the verb in sentence C? _____

Sentence A is written in the *active voice*. In the active voice, the subject performs the action of the verb. Sentences B and C are written in the *passive voice*. In the passive voice, the subject receives the action of the verb, or is acted upon.

You probably noticed that the sentence written in the active voice is shorter and more direct. Its verb is a single word, an action verb. Although the meaning does not change significantly in sentences B and C, certain characteristics distinguish passive voice. The sentences written in the passive voice are slightly longer; they contain verb phrases and sometimes a prepositional phrase (which names who completed the action).

7. What is the helping verb in sentences B and C? _____

8. What is the prepositional phrase that states who completed the action in sentence B?

_____

Label the following sentences AV if they are written in the active voice and PV if they are written in the passive voice.

_____ 1. JoAnn made pizza.

_____ 2. The pizza was made by JoAnn.

_____ 3. It was recommended by the superintendent that all middle school students wear uniforms.

_____ 4. The superintendent recommended that all middle school students wear uniforms.

_____ 5. This year's performance by the band members surpassed previous standards.

_____ 6. The band performed extremely well this year.

_____ 7. Mistakes in the document were corrected as quickly as possible.

_____ 8. A serious effort was made to avoid the same types of mistakes in the future.

Recognizing Choices

Active or Passive Voice?
Choose the active voice when you want to be direct and powerful. You will want to choose the active voice when
1) you want to emphasize the subject (who performs the action).
example: Elizabeth won the middle-school regional spelling bee.
2) you want a short, clear sentence.
example: We need help!

Think of a situation in which you would want to know who performed the action of the sentence or in which you would want to use a short sentence. Write the situation below. Share your situation with your classmates and compile a class list of situations in which choosing the active voice is appropriate.

_____

*Answers to page 23: 1. John, 2. published, 3. Research, 4. was published, 5. research, 6. was published, 7. was, 8. by John

Although many writers use the active voice more often, the passive voice is useful in many circumstances. It is a good choice when

1) you do not know who performs the action or it does not matter.
   example: The statistics have been compiled.
2) you do not want the reader to know who the performer is.
   example: A mistake was made in filling out your order.
3) you want to emphasize the action and not the performer.
   example: The city's drinking water is becoming polluted.

Think of a situation in which you may not know who performed the action, you do not want your reader to know who performed the action, or you want to emphasize the action and not the performer. Write that situation below. Share your situation with your classmates and compile a class list of situations in which choosing the passive voice is appropriate.

_____

The choice between active and passive voice depends upon what you want to say. Read the following pairs of sentences. One is written in the active voice, and the other is written in the passive voice. Determine which voice is the better choice by circling A or B. Be ready to explain why your choice is the better one.

1 - A. Theresa Martin in our billing department overcharged Mr. Joseph Thompson's account $396.98.
1 - B. Mr. Joseph Thompson's account was inadvertently overcharged $396.98.

2 - A. Sharon Gunderson broke the school record for the most points scored in a high-school career in basketball with a four-year total of 1,062 points.
2 - B. The school record for the most points scored in a high-school career in basketball was broken by Sharon Gunderson's four-year total of 1,062 points.

3 - A. Word-processing assignments should always be saved on a back-up disk!
3 - B. My friend tells me to always save word-processing assignments on a back-up disk!

4 - A. Members of the science class hypothesized that a repetition of the experiment would produce the same results.
4 - B. It was hypothesized by members of the science class that a repetition of the experiment would produce the same results.

5 - A. "We must leave as quickly as possible," was uttered by Samantha.
5 - B. "We must leave as quickly as possible," Samantha uttered.

*Answers to page 24: 1. AV, 2. PV, 3. PV, 4. AV, 5. AV, 6. AV, 7. PV, 8. PV

Making Choices

Select one of the following writing situations. First write mainly in the passive voice. Then write the same assignment in the active voice.

- an informative paragraph discussing the benefits of regular exercise
- an informative paragraph discussing the dangers of dieting
- a letter to the editor of the local newspaper praising the city's efforts to raise money to build a new teen center
- a letter notifying a customer that the prom dress she ordered was lost during shipment and will not be available for her prom
- an advertisement praising the value of SkyRocket athletic shoes
- a letter firing an employee who has worked for the Perfect Candle Company for ten years.
- a plot summary of a memorable book or movie
- a summary of an experiment on plant growth in various types of soils

Active Voice

_____

_____

_____

_____

_____

Passive Voice

_____

_____

_____

_____

_____

_____

Share your two versions with a classmate. Discuss the following questions. Which was easier to write, the active or passive voice? Which was more effective? Why?

*Answers to page 25: 1. B, 2. A, 3. A, 4. A, 5. B

Selecting Levels of Formality

Understanding Choices

Although we write for different audiences, purposes, and occasions, all the writing we do basically falls into three levels of formality—conversational, informal, and formal. Our intended audience and our purpose for writing determine the most suitable level.

Conversational

One level of writing is the conversational level (some people call it the colloquial level). Writing done at this level reflects the language we use every day with our closest friends. Little attention is paid to the conventions of standard grammar. The conversational level is marked by the following characteristics:

- many contractions
- slang (often including local or regional dialect)
- familiar words
- sentence fragments
- short sentences (fewer than 12 words)
- many simple sentences
- use of "I" or "you"
- short paragraphs (five to seven sentences)

The expression "a hot set of wheels" is written at the conversational level. Similarly, the sentences, "Let's chow down this pizza, pronto!" and "Hi! How ya' doin'?" are written at the conversational level. Not all sentences at the conversational level contain slang or contractions. For example, the sentence "I can be ready in an hour" also is a conversational, or colloquial, sentence.

1. On what writing occasion(s) would it be acceptable to use a conversational level?

_____

2. For what audience(s) would it be acceptable? _____

3. Write an original sentence at the conversational level._____

_____

Informal

The informal level of usage shows more formality than the conversational level. Writing done at this level retains some characteristics of the conversational level, but pays more attention to standard conventions of grammar and is understood by most readers. You would use the informal level when the audience is less familiar or when you would like to show respect. Here are characteristics of informal writing.

- contractions
- some slang (depending upon audience and purpose)
- some polysyllabic words
- complete sentences
- simple and compound (even some complex) sentences
- somewhat longer sentence length
- use of *I* or *you* (when referring to readers) acceptable
- longer paragraphs

Examples of this level of writing are "the fastest car on the road" and "Let's eat the pizza fast so that we can make the movie." Because differences may be slight, occasionally you may feel that a sentence is both conversational and informal.

1. On what occasion(s) would it be acceptable to use the informal level of writing?

    _____

    _____

2. For what audience(s) would this level be appropriate? _____

3. Write an original sentence at the informal level. _____

    _____

Neither the conversational level nor the informal level should be confused with nonstandard usage. *Nonstandard* usage includes errors that are very obvious and that are never considered acceptable. An example of nonstandard usage follows: John ain't gots no money. Notice that nonstandard usage is different from the slang and contractions that characterize conversational and informal levels of writing; nonstandard words and phrases are incorrect in any type of communication.

Formal

The formal level of writing is used when you do not know your audience or when you want to show utmost respect. This level of writing reflects careful preparation and strict adherence to standard conventions. Qualities of formal writing include the following:

- no contractions
- no slang
- many polysyllabic words
- avoidance of using *you*
- use of *I* or *we* only acceptable in some cases
- longer sentences
- many compound, complex, and compound-complex sentences
- may contain long, involved paragraphs

1. On what occasion(s) would it be appropriate to use the formal level of writing?

_____

2. For what audience(s) would formal writing be acceptable? _____

3. Write an original sentence at the formal level. _____

_____

Write your conversational, informal, and formal sentences on three separate strips of paper. Your classmates will do the same. Place all the strips in a box. Each student will then randomly select three of the strips and will write the level of the sentence on the back of the sentence strip.

Hold a class discussion about the different sentences. Compare all the sentences written at the conversational level. Count the words of several sentences. Notice the slang and contractions. Are certain words and phrases repeated? Now, compare all the sentences written at the informal level. Count the words of several of these sentences. Notice contractions and polysyllabic words. Are any of the informal sentences compound or complex? Finally, compare all the sentences written at the formal level. Count the words of several of these sentences. How many formal sentences are either compound, complex, or compound-complex?

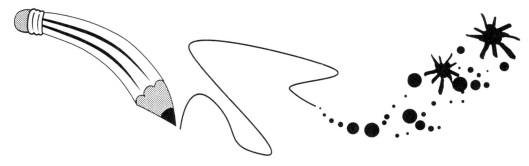

Recognizing Choices

Which Level of Formality?

To be able to write at all three levels of formality, you first need to recognize the characteristics of each level. The choice often depends on how well you know your audience and the degree of respect you wish to show your audience. The chart below shows audiences and occasions for writing. Identify each of the following levels by filling in the blanks with "conversational," "informal," and "formal."

Level of Formality	Audience	Occasion
_____	close friends, family members	impromptu notes, messages, journal entries
_____	acquaintances, teachers, friends	letters, informal school essays
_____	general, unknown audience; prospective business client or employer	research papers, news articles, textbooks, business correspondence

Which level do the following words and phrases represent? Write a "C" for conversational level, an "I" for informal level, and an "F" for formal level.

_____ 1. communicate

_____ 2. talk

_____ 3. blab

_____ 4. subsequently

_____ 5. when

_____ 6. we regret to inform you

_____ 7. I can't attend your party.

_____ 8. Hey, man! That's cool.

_____ 9. Please reply in writing.

_____ 10. No way!

Which level of formality would you use in the following writing situations? Write a "C" for conversational level, an "I" for informal level, and an "F" for formal level. More than one level may be appropriate in some instances.

_____ 1. an application for a college scholarship

_____ 2. note to your best friend complaining about a tough social studies assignment

_____ 3. thank-you card for a graduation gift from your elderly neighbor

_____ 4. letter to the editor of *Science Quarterly* magazine

_____ 5. message to your mother reminding her to buy several items for your
_____ slumber party

_____ 6. essay for language arts class about a personal experience

_____ 7. a 20-page research paper with a works cited page

_____ 8. proposal to the middle school principal to have a student council dance

You will notice as you move from the conversational to the formal level that the tone becomes less personal. Once you select a level, make every effort to use words, phrases, and sentences that fit the occasion and audience.

The following letter contains many sentences that are written at the conversational level, which is too informal for its purpose. Revise this paragraph, making it more appropriate for a formal level of communication.

Dear Aaron:

Thanks a lot for applying to Sunset University! Many real good students applied this year. We've looked at your transcripts and recommendations. We feel that we can't accept you into our university this year. We regret to let you know that you weren't chosen. We'd like to have you try again next year. Please apply again next year between February 1 and May 15. We wish you lots of success in trying to find a college. I'll look forward to seeing your application next year.

Clifford Nolton
Office of Admissions

*Answers to page 30: conversational, informal, formal 1. F, 2. I, 3. C, 4. F, 5. C or I, 6. F, 7. I, 8. C, 9. F, 10. C

Name _____

Making Choices

Friendly Letter: You are writing a note to a friend thanking her for the invitation to spend a week at her lakeside cottage. You cannot wait to visit her and will accept the invitation. What level of formality will you use? _____

Why? _____

Letter of Complaint: You recently purchased a new CD player. However, when you first turn it on, there is static, the player skips, and then the unit quits. After the unit warms up, the CDs play fine. You would like to return the CD player for repairs at no cost to you or exchange the CD player for a different one. What level of formality will you use?
_____

Why? _____

Research Paper for Science: You have conducted an experiment on the effects of different soils on growing soybeans. Your data covers a two-month period. Your research findings will be presented to a panel of science professors from the state university, and they will determine the winner of a $5,000.00 scholarship. You need to write a two-paragraph summary of your research project. Which level of formality will you use? _____

Why? _____

School Announcement: As president of the student council, you must post a flier encouraging all students to attend the spring clean-up of the city parks. After the work is completed, the student council will sponsor a dance and pizza party for students who have worked. Which level of formality will you use? _____

Why? _____

Personal Note: You taped a short note on the locker of a close friend asking him to meet you after school for pizza. Which level of formality will you use? _____

Why? _____

Select one of the above writing situations and complete that assignment using the most appropriate level of formality.

*Answers to page 31: 1. F, 2. C or I, 3. I or F, 4. F, 5. C or I, 6. I, 7. F, 8. I or F

Measuring Readability

Understanding Choices

People who publish books and magazines pay close attention to what they call the "readability" of their stories and articles. You do the same thing. Depending on your audience, you select the words—and even the types of sentences—that you think will be most easily understood by your readers. For example, if you were writing a story for someone in the primary grades, you would choose simple words and short sentences. On the other hand, if you were writing to your teacher, you would choose bigger words and longer sentences.

1. Which of the following sentences would you rate the most difficult? Place "1" in the blank for the most difficult, "2" for average difficulty, and "3" for the least difficult.

   _____ A. Understanding well the importance of exercise in winter months, Ramon decided to take up the sport of cross-country skiing.

   _____ B. Ramon liked cross-country skiing as a way to exercise in winter.

   _____ C. Because cross-country skiing offers aerobic, as well as cardiac benefits, Ramon was resolute in his determination to pursue this sport religiously during the winter months.

2. Sometimes reading difficulty occurs because the reader simply does not know all of the words. What words, if any, did you find unfamiliar? _____
   _____

3. Reading difficulty can also be affected by the length of words and sentences. Short sentences are not necessarily simple, nor are long ones necessarily difficult, but in general, shorter words and sentences are easier to read. Compare the word and sentence length of the above sentences.

	Number of Words in the Sentence	Number of Words with Three or More Syllables
Least Difficult	_____	_____
Average Difficulty	_____	_____
Most Difficult	_____	_____

Recognizing Choices

The following passages were written for three different audiences. On the lines below, identify the passage you find least difficult, of average difficulty, and most difficult.

Passage #1 _____

He pushed the door open and stepped inside. Then for a full minute he did not move. He shivered and lifted his eyes from the figure and looked around the small room. The stove shone black in the sunlight which the open door let in. On the table, covered with white oilcloth, the loaf of gingerbread lay uncovered; beside it lay a knife used to cut off the piece which the man on the floor had not eaten before he died. Nothing else was disturbed. Nothing else seemed in the least to bear any evidence of what had taken place.

Passage #2 _____

About this time, I met with an odd volume of the *Spectator*. I thought the writing excellent, and wished, if possible, to imitate it. I took some of the papers, and, making short hints of the sentiment in each sentence, I laid them by a few days, and then, without looking at the book, tried to complete the papers again, by expressing each hinted sentiment at length, as fully as it had been expressed before, in any suitable words that should come to hand. Then I compared my Spectator with the original, discovered some of my faults, and corrected them.

Passage #3 _____

Once upon a time there was a small boy. He had just finished eating an apple. He threw what was left of the apple down to the ground and walked off. This apple just happened to be my great, great, granddad. Out of the remains of the apple grew a giant apple tree. This tree was where I spent most of my life. I was very happy living on the tree with all of my relatives. We rarely lost a member to a hungry passerby. My spot on the tree was at the very top. I could see for miles.

Passage #1 was written for adolescents (*Jean of the Lazy A*, by B. M. Bower); passage #2 for adults (Ben Franklin's *Autobiography*); and passage #3 for children ("The Apple Tree Family" by a middle school student). Count the number of sentences in each passage. Then count the number of words with three or more syllables, and record the numbers below. See whether easier passages have shorter words and sentences. Passage #1 has been done for you.

	Passage #1	Passage #2	Passage #3
Number of Sentences	7		
Number of Words with 3 or More Syllables	3		

Readability Formulas

Although counting syllables and sentences cannot guarantee clear and effective sentences, it can alert you to possible problems. To help writers think about the audience's needs, some people have developed systems for measuring reading difficulty based on the length of words and sentences. Below is a typical formula (slightly simplified). Use this formula to calculate and compare the readability scores of the three passages on the previous page. The most difficult reading passage should have the highest readability score.

(The first step in the formula is to count 100 words. Each of the reading passages has exactly 100 words.) Passage #1 has been done for you.

Passage #1: _____14_____ + _____3_____ = _____17_____
              Average Sentence Length   Percent of Long Words   Readability Score

Passage #2: _____ + _____ = _____
              Average Sentence Length   Percent of Long Words   Readability Score

Passage #3: _____ + _____ = _____
              Average Sentence Length   Percent of Long Words   Readability Score

Readability Formula

(1) Select a passage of 100 words.

(2) Find the <u>Average Sentence Length</u> by dividing the number of words by the number of sentences.

_____ ÷ _____ = _____
(Number of Words)   (Number of Sentences)   (Average Sentence Length)

(3) Find the <u>Percent of Long Words</u> by dividing the number of long words (3 or more syllables) by 100.

_____ ÷ 100 = _____
(Number of Long Words)   (Percent of Long Words)

(4) Find the <u>Readability Score</u> by adding the Average Sentence Length and the Percent of Long Words. (Higher scores suggest greater reading difficulty.)

_____ + _____ = _____
(Average Sentence Length) (Percent of Long Words)   (Readability Score)

Making Choices

1. In his *Autobiography,* Benjamin Franklin said that he learned to write by imitating the writing in a magazine he admired, the *Spectator*. He even created his own version of the magazine. In a story of at least 100 words, describe an experience you had learning to read or write. Direct your story (true or fictional) to an audience of primary school students.

2. Use the formula to calculate the readability score for your story. If your story is shorter than 100 words, you can still determine the readability by following these steps:

    (1) Count the number of words.
    (2) Count the number of sentences.
    (3) Divide the number of words by the number of sentences to find the <u>Average Sentence Length.</u>
    (4) Count the number of long words (three or more syllables).
    (5) Divide the number of long words by the total number of words in the story to find the <u>Percent of Long Words.</u>
    (6) Add the <u>Average Sentence Length</u> and the <u>Percent of Long Words</u>.

3. Rewrite your story for a PTA newsletter. Your purpose is to help parents and teachers understand the kinds of activities that are most helpful for students learning to read and write. If you wish, include information about what you did not find helpful.

4. Calculate the readability of your second story. Record and compare the scores of your two stories. Do your readability scores show that you have taken into consideration the different reading abilities of your audiences?

Story Title	Intended Audience	Readability Score
	Primary School Students	
	Parent-Teacher Association	

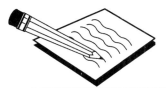

CHAPTER 3
Organizing Ideas

Using Subject-Verb Order

Understanding Choices

Readers expect to see subjects first and verbs second. They also expect that the subjects will be performing the actions and the verbs will be naming the actions. Readers learn this pattern in their earliest days in school. Although other patterns are helpful in providing variety and emphasizing particular information, they are not as easy to read.

Look at the following pairs of sentences. Circle the one in each pair that you find easier to read.

1. The plan of the girls was to go on a camping trip.   2. The girls planned a camping trip.
3. The music was enjoyed by the students.   4. The students enjoyed the music.
5. There was dissatisfaction among the students about the food.   6. Students disliked the food.

Most readers would find sentences 2, 4, and 6 easiest to read because
- they follow subject-verb order.
- the subjects perform the actions and the verbs name the actions.

In the blank lines below, identify the subjects and verbs for sentences 2, 4, and 6 above.

	Subject	**Verb**
2.	_____	_____
4.	_____	_____
6.	_____	_____

Identify the subjects and verbs for sentences 1, 3, and 5. Notice that they show no one performing an action.

1.	_____	_____
3.	_____	_____
5.	_____	_____

As you saw on the previous page, the sentences that were easiest to read had the subjects performing the actions and the verbs naming the actions. Now look at the patterns that were not quite so easy. None of them is grammatically incorrect. In fact, sometimes they may be a better choice—they can emphasize a point or provide variety. However, because they are not as easy to read, they probably should be used sparingly.

Sentence #1: "The plan of the girls was to go on a camping trip" uses *plan* as the subject and the linking verb *was* as the verb. This pattern eliminates the action and requires more words. The sentence below follows the same pattern. Revise it to create an actor-action sequence in which the subject performs the action and the verb names the action.

Cheri and Judy's plan was to drive to Alaska with four friends.

_____

How many words are in the original sentence? _____ In your revised sentence? _____

Sentence #3: "The music was enjoyed by the students" uses a passive construction in which *music* is the subject and *was enjoyed* is the verb. This pattern removes the actor (*students*) from the subject position and requires more words. The sentence below follows the same pattern. Revise it to create an actor-action sequence in which the subject performs the action and the verb names the action.

The camping gear was assembled by Dave and Bob.

_____

How many words are in the original sentence? _____ In your revised sentence? _____

Sentence #5: "There was dissatisfaction among the students about the food" uses a *there was* construction in which *dissatisfaction* is the subject and *was* is the verb. This pattern removes the actor (*students*) from the subject position and adds words. The sentence below follows the same pattern. Revise it to create an actor-action sequence in which the subject performs the action and the verb names the action.

There was a great wish among the travelers to begin their excellent adventure as soon as possible.

_____

_____

How many words are in the original sentence? _____ In your revised sentence? _____

Recognizing Choices

Sometimes writers deliberately choose passive constructions, linking verbs, and *there was* constructions, depending on the point they want to make. For example, fairy tales often begin quite effectively with a *there was* construction, which emphasizes whatever words follow it. Notice in the first sentence below that the *there was* construction emphasizes *a very powerful queen*. How does this emphasis change in each of the other sentences? Match the letter with the sentence.

    a. Someone (we are not told who) kept the queen's subjects illiterate.
    b. Subjects were illiterate. We are not told why.
    c. The queen forced the subjects to remain illiterate.

       1. Once upon a time **there was** a very powerful queen, who kept all of her subjects illiterate.

_____ 2. Once upon a time a powerful queen **kept** all of her subjects illiterate. (actor-action)

_____ 3. Once upon a time a powerful queen's subjects **were kept** illiterate. (passive)

_____ 4. Once upon a time a powerful queen's subjects **were** illiterate. (linking)

Read the following passage from a student paper about similarities and differences in the book and movie *Old Yeller*. In the space above the sentence, rewrite the underlined sentences to create an actor-action sequence. Discuss whether the change is an improvement or not. The first passage is done for you.

    The book and movie *Old Yeller* have many similarities and differences. (1) In both the

        Old Mr. Sanderson owns the same Yeller dog.
book and the movie, <u>it is the same Yeller dog owned by old Mr. Sanderson.</u> Travis also

gets a horse in both, and he gets hurt. Another similarity in both is that LisiBeth stays

behind when Travis is hurt.

    In the movie (2) <u>Yeller was penned up by the family</u> before they killed him, but in the

book they killed him right away. (3) In the movie <u>Arlis was given an Indian headdress by

Pa.</u> Ma got a dress. When Travis went to mark the pigs, he stood on an embankment in

the book, but in the movie (4) <u>it was a tree limb that he climbed out on.</u>

Making Choices

Working in pairs, write the first draft of a movie review for classmates. Like Siskel and Ebert, begin by briefly summarizing the story. Then evaluate the story line, acting quality, and special effects. Conclude by giving a "thumbs up" or "thumbs down" and ranking the movie with zero to four stars. Revise your movie review to use actor-action patterns where appropriate.

Movie Title: _____

Summary: _____

_____

_____

_____

_____

_____

_____

_____

Evaluation: _____

_____

_____

_____

_____

_____

_____

_____

_____

Thumbs Up: ____ **Down:** ____   **Rating:** _____

Using Cue Words to Guide the Reader

As you have seen, there are many different ways of saying the same thing, but your purpose and audience determine how you say it. It is important to remember that your readers want to understand you. They assume that your writing makes sense, and they will put forth every effort to see that it does. In fact, they will often fill in missing information. But if the words are not appropriate, or if they are not in a predictable pattern, your readers may feel that the job is just too difficult. However, if you have (1) arranged the content in a familiar pattern and (2) provided signposts along the way to help them make connections, they will be able to stay with you until the end. Think of these signposts, or cue words, as taking your reader by the hand and saying, "Let me show you the way."

Understanding Choices

Readers expect to find familiar patterns in what they read and are confused if their expectations are not met. You know about these patterns, even if you can't name them, because you hear them when people speak, you read them in books and magazines, and you use them when you think. Notice that each of the following word groups suggests a pattern for a whole paragraph or more.

Write a sentence continuing each idea.

1. Once upon a time there was a _____

_____

2. The accident could have been avoided if _____

_____

3. Movie popcorn tastes better than store popcorn because _____

_____

You probably had no difficulty developing these thoughts because you recognized the familiar patterns. Which word group suggested a pattern of

_____ cause/effect?

_____ comparison/contrast?

_____ chronological order?

Cues that Signal Structure

1. In the first example on the previous page, you probably began a story in chronological order. In the second, you talked about the cause of the accident, and in the third about differences between the two types of popcorn. You did this because you recognized the various structural patterns: chronological order, cause/effect, and comparison/contrast. These are common patterns that we draw on many times a day in speaking, listening, writing, and reading. We recognize these patterns partly through the content itself and partly through cue words. The following passage provides cue words to help the reader predict what will happen next:

> Early one morning a fisherman made a very successful cast and brought in a great lot of fish with his net. Soon, however, . . .

What do you predict will happen? _____

What cue word(s) caused you to make this prediction? _____

2. Conjunctions are some of the most common cue words that we use. They tell whether a second idea should be added *(and)*, contrasted *(but, yet)*, seen as a cause *(for)*, or seen as an alternative *(or)*. If no cue word is given, the reader assumes that the second idea adds to or explains the first. Look at the three pairs of sentences below. One pair needs no cue word because the second sentence explains the first sentence. One pair needs to be joined by *but* to show contrast, and one pair needs *and* to show that a new point is added. In the space in front of each pair, write the word that best joins the pair. If no word is needed, write *none*.

_____ 1. My little brother is cute. He is very smart.

_____ 2. My little brother is cute. He has a bad temper.

_____ 3. My little brother is cute. He has dark, curly hair and sparkling eyes.

3. Words like *first, second, next,* and *finally* signal chronological order; words like *however* and *on the other hand* signal contrast; and words like *consequently* and *as a result* signal cause/effect relationships. Look at the following three pairs of sentences. On the blank line, write *In fact, On the other hand,* and *As a result* in the appropriate lines.

_____ a. Pizza is my favorite food. I can be quite happy with tacos.

_____ b. Pizza is my favorite food. I could eat it for every meal.

_____ c. Pizza is my favorite food. I have to exercise to burn the calories.

Cues that Show Writers' Attitudes

Some cue words tell how writers feel about what they say. If they say "clearly," they are really telling the reader, "Believe me, this is true." If they say "perhaps," they are alerting the reader that they are not quite so certain. In the following examples, notice that the main content of the sentence remains the same, but the cue words cause the sentences to convey quite different messages. Which statement is most certain about the benefits of vitamin C? Which statement is least certain? Write "most certain" and "least certain" in the appropriate blanks.

_____ 1. If you take your vitamin C, you **may** not catch a cold.

_____ 2. If you take your vitamin C, you **probably** will not catch a cold.

_____ 3. If you take your vitamin C, you **almost certainly** will not catch a cold.

Cues that Identify Writers' Intentions

Sometimes cues tell readers directly what a writer intends to do or has done. Look at the italicized cues in the following examples.

a. *In the next section, I will explain* exactly how I plan to solve the behavior problem at the movie theater.

b. *You may be asking yourself, "Why is this a problem?" Let me explain.* People cannot hear if others are talking while the film is playing, and food spilled on the seats can damage clothing.

_____ 1. Which sentence(s) suggests what is coming next?

_____ 2. Which sentence(s) refers both to what has gone on before and what is to come?

Avoiding Excessive Use of Cues

Although all of these cue words can make reading easier, too many cue words can make reading more difficult. Compare these two sentences.

a. *In my opinion, however,* I see no *obvious* reason to do this.
b. *However,* I see no reason to do this.

1. Explain why the phrase *In my opinion* is not necessary. _____

2. Explain why the word *obvious* is not necessary. _____

Recognizing Choices

The passage below from Mark Twain's Preface to *Tom Sawyer* has cue words or phrases removed. Some of the cue words help the reader to predict the structure, and others show the writer's attitude or intention. See whether you can choose the correct cue words and write them in the appropriate blanks. (The answers are at the bottom of the following page.)

Most of	Although	to try	but	mainly
I hope	part of	for	really	pleasantly

_____ the adventures recorded in this book _____ occurred; one or two

were experiences of my own, the rest those of boys who were schoolmates of mine. Huck

Finn is drawn from life; Tom Sawyer also, _____ not from an individual—he is a

combination of the characteristics of three boys whom I knew. _____ my book is

intended _____ for the entertainment of boys and girls, _____ it will not be

shunned by men and women on that account, _____ _____ my plan

has been _____ to _____ remind adults of what they once were

themselves, and of how they felt and thought and talked.

Below is the same passage without the cue words. Read both passages out loud. What effect do the cue words have?

> The adventures recorded in this book occurred; one or two were experiences of my own, the rest those of boys who were schoolmates of mine. Huck Finn is drawn from life; Tom Sawyer also, not from an individual—he is a combination of the characteristics of three boys whom I knew. My book is intended for the entertainment of boys and girls. It will not be shunned by men and women on that account. My plan has been to remind adults of what they once were themselves, and of how they felt and thought and talked.

The following sentences contain too many cue words. Work with a partner to cross out words that you feel make the reading more difficult. Compare your changes with those of other classmates, and explain your choices.

a. In conclusion, I would like to point out that, finally, the decision has to be the student's.
b. But on the other hand, students, I believe, probably need to understand that rules are necessary.
c. It is my belief that, eventually, it may turn out to be a case of mistaken identity.

Making Choices

Cue Words that Signal Structure

Write a story about an unusual person in your neighborhood when you were a child. The story can be true or fictional. As you tell your story, use at least five words from the following list of structural cues. (Note: If the cue is to be helpful, the reader needs to have it early in the sentence, probably within the first six words.) Circle the cues that you use in the story.

As a result	For example	In fact	Similarly
Another	For this reason	In other words	On the other hand
Besides	Furthermore	In spite of this	Therefore
Consequently	However	Otherwise	Until then
Finally	In addition	Meanwhile	Because of this

An Unusual Person in My Neighborhood

When I was little, a very unusual person lived in my neighborhood. _____

_____

_____

_____

_____

_____

_____

_____

_____

_____

Read your story to classmates in small groups, first with the cue words and then without them. Discuss the effect that the cue words have on the understanding and enjoyment of the stories.

*Answer, page 44: *Most of* the adventures recorded in this book *really* occurred; one or two were experiences of my own, the rest those of boys who were schoolmates of mine. Huck Finn is drawn from life; Tom Sawyer also, *but* not from an individual—he is a combination of the characteristics of three boys whom I knew. *Although* my book is intended *mainly* for the entertainment of boys and girls, *I hope* it will not be shunned by men and women on that account, *for part of* my plan has been *to try* to *pleasantly* remind adults of what they once were themselves, and of how they felt and thought and talked.

Cue Words that Signal the Writer's Attitude and Intentions

Write a short essay describing a teacher that you recall fondly from an early grade in school. Use at least five words or phrases from the list of words below, signaling (1) your attitude toward what you are writing and (2) your intentions as you write. Circle the cues that you use.

Apparently	Similarly	Of course
In my opinion	I say this because	Certainly
Perhaps	It is unlikely	Obviously
It seems that	I want to point out	I hope you don't think
Incidentally	Clearly	I truly believe
Before I describe	In some ways	Without a doubt

My Favorite Teacher

My favorite teacher in _____ grade was _____

_____

_____

_____

_____

_____

_____

_____

_____

_____

_____

_____

Read your story to classmates in small groups, first with the cue words and then without them. Discuss the effect that the cue words have on the understanding and enjoyment of the stories.

Connecting New Information to Old

Understanding Choices

Whenever you learn something new, you connect the new information to something you already know. For example, if you were told that an Olympic runner had just broken a record, you would know immediately that the runner had run faster than anyone else. Not for a minute would you think that the runner had smashed a musical "platter." You would know this because of the knowledge you have about Olympics, running, and sports records. On the other hand, if you were told that iambic pentameter is more common than trochaic tetrameter, the information would be meaningless unless you knew something about various metrical patterns in poetry.

Creating Emphasis with Old-New Sequence

As a writer, you must keep in mind that your readers also need to connect new information to old. As they read, they predict what comes next based on what they already know and what the writer has told them. Whenever possible, help your readers by following these guidelines:

- **Put familiar information at the beginning of the sentence.**
- **Put new information (what you want to emphasize) at the end of the sentence.**

Look at the following sentences and predict what the writer will talk about next. Circle the appropriate letter, and write a sentence that could follow.

1. River City has some beautiful new buildings, but it also has several unsightly areas. What kind of information do you predict will come next?
   (a) information about beautiful buildings (b) information about unsightly areas

   _____

   _____

2. River City has several unsightly areas, but it also has some beautiful new buildings. What kind of information do you predict will come next?
   (a) information about beautiful buildings (b) information about unsightly areas

   _____

   _____

Most readers would choose "b" for sentence 1 and "a" for sentence 2. By placing these topics last in the sentence, the writer has signaled that they are the new or important information.

Connecting Old and New with Topic Words

In addition to using the old-new sequence, you can help your reader to make connections between different pieces of information by repeating the topic word (or some word that refers to it) from time to time. For example, if you were going to write about the popularity of in-line skating, you might begin with a sentence like this:

> In-line skating has become popular with young and old alike.

In this sentence, you have announced that your main topic is *In-line skating*. In the second part of the sentence, you have announced that you will also be talking about its *popularity* with *young and old*. If you continued with more information about in-line skating's popularity, you might write something like this:

> In-line skating has become popular with young and old alike. However, these groups see the benefits of the sport differently. Young people are attracted to its speed, whereas older people see it as a great way to exercise.

Notice how the writer has used synonyms and pronouns to remind the reader of the topics introduced in the first sentence. In the following blanks, tell whether each word or phrase at the left refers to *in-line skating* or *young and old*.

these groups _____ its _____

sport _____ older people _____

young people _____ it _____

You probably had no difficulty seeing that *these groups*, *young people*, and *older people* remind readers of *young and old*, whereas *sport*, *its*, and *it* remind them of *in-line skating*.

A second way to help readers make connections between new and old, then, is to

- **Repeat topic words (or words that refer to them) from time to time.**

Using the passage above as a model, write three sentences about a favorite sport. Put new information last in the sentence and repeat topic words (or substitutes) from time to time.

_____

_____

_____

Recognizing Choices

Working in pairs, place the sentences below in the order that you think best follows the first sentence. In making your choices, look especially at the old-new sequences. Put the numbers "1," "2," and "3" in the blanks in front of the appropriate sentences. If you feel that a sentence does not fit, place "0" in the blank. Explain the reasons for your choices. (Likely responses are on the following page.)

In-line skates are fun, but they are also dangerous.

_____ a. Hockey teams are springing up in neighborhoods across the country.

_____ b. Minimal equipment includes a helmet, knee pads, and arm and wrist pads.

_____ c. Thousands of people are injured needlessly each year.

_____ d. Many of these injuries could easily be avoided with a few items of safety apparel.

Now compare two passages, both with similar information. One follows the old-new sequence; the other does not.

1. One of our most popular magazines—which introduced a relatively new concept to the American magazine market—is *People* magazine, selling millions of copies each week. As a result of *People's* financial success, *Newsweek* and *Time* have expanded their own feature sections on famous personalities.

2. One of our most popular magazines—selling millions of copies each week—is *People* magazine, which introduced a relatively new concept to the American magazine market. *Newsweek* and *Time* have expanded their own feature sections on famous personalities as a result of *People's* financial success.

In passage 1, what topic is emphasized at the end of the first sentence? _____

What topic is mentioned at the beginning of the second sentence? _____

In passage 2, what topic is emphasized at the end of the first sentence? _____

What topic is mentioned at the beginning of the second sentence? _____

Which passage follows the old-new sequence and repeats topic words? _____

Revising a Rough Draft to Make Connections

You will not actually think about these guidelines as you write because you will want to focus on getting your ideas down on paper. Instead, you will think about these strategies during revision. Eventually, you will begin to use them naturally as you write. Below is the beginning paragraph of a student essay. Answer the questions below, and revise the paragraph to make it clearer.

Growing Up

(1) Every teenager wants to grow up to become an adult. (2) Testing parents and pushing the limits becomes a way of life. (3) An inch gained is a step into the real world, a world independent of parents and authority. (4) As young people gain this independence, they feel that a world of opportunity awaits them. (5) However, as they age, they come to realize that maturity can also bring suffering and pain.

1. Read the first sentence: "Every teenager wants to grow up to become an adult."

   What would you expect to come next? _____

2. Look at the second sentence. Does it do what you predicted? _____
   Although you can figure out what the reader probably meant, the old-new connection is not there. How might you revise these two sentences to make better connections?

   _____

   _____

3. Here is one of many possible way to revise these sentences.

   Because teenagers want to grow to adulthood quickly, they are constantly <u>testing their parents.</u> Pushing the limits becomes a way of life.

   What words in the second sentence connect to the idea in the first sentence of *testing parents?*

   _____

*Answers, page 49: a. 0; b. 3; c. 1; d. 2.

Here is a revised version of the paragraph. Look at the old-new and topic-reference connections, and fill in the appropriate words in the blanks below.

Growing Up

(1) Because <u>teenagers</u> want to grow to adulthood quickly, <u>they</u> are constantly <u>testing their</u> parents. (2) <u>Pushing the limits</u> becomes a way of life. (3) <u>An inch gained</u> is a step into the adult world, a world <u>independent</u> of parents and authority. (4) As <u>young people</u> gain <u>this independence</u>, <u>they</u> feel that a world of opportunity awaits <u>them</u>. (5) However, as <u>they</u> age, <u>they</u> come to realize that maturity can also bring suffering and pain.

1. *An inch gained* in sentence 3 continues the connection to *testing* in sentence 1 and

   _____ in sentence 2.

2. *This independence* in sentence 4 connects to _____ in sentence 3.

3. *They* in sentence 5 connects to _____ in sentence 4.

4. What two pronouns in sentence 4 refer to *young people?* _____ _____

5. What two pronouns in sentence 5 refer to *young people?* _____ _____

6. What do you predict the writer would talk about next? _____

   _____

7. Write several sentences continuing the paragraph. Try to maintain old-new connections.

   _____

   _____

   _____

   _____

8. Exchange paragraphs with your partner and identify connecting words and ideas.

Making Choices

Write an essay or a story on the following topic.

Imagine that your television viewing has been restricted to three hours a week. What shows would you watch and why? You may divide the time any way you want—several half-hour shows, one long movie, or a variety of news, sports, and drama programs.

Help your readers by using old-new sequences and repeated topic words. When introducing a new, important term, arrange the sentence so that the new term comes toward the end. Even if you have to create an additional sentence to do this, the clarity is usually worth it. Sometimes you may want to break long sentences into shorter ones, exposing information you want to emphasize.

Exchange papers and answer the questions below.

Peer Response Sheet

1. **Read the title.** Predict what the essay will be about.

2. **Read the introductory paragraph.** Now what do you predict the essay will be about?

3. **Read the body of the essay, including the headings.** As you read each paragraph, predict what will come next. Then tell whether the writer developed the point you expected. Mark any passage that you find confusing or unclear.

4. **Read the title, the introduction, and the headings again.** Write a brief conclusion for the essay.

5. **Read the conclusion.** Compare your conclusion with that of the writer.

6. **Reread the essay, sentence by sentence.** Look at those areas you marked earlier as unclear. See whether connecting information—old-new sequences, repeated topic words, and references to topics—could make them clearer.

7. Discuss your responses with the author.

Choosing Organizational Patterns

Understanding Choices

The organizational patterns that you choose when you write are always determined by what you want to say. If you want to show similarities or differences, you would choose comparison/contrast; if you want to show the effects of something, you might choose cause/effect; if you have ideas about how to solve a problem, you would use a problem/solution pattern; and if you want to describe a place, you would use spatial order. These patterns apply both to the overall organizational plan of a whole document and to the sentences and groups of sentences within the document. Imagine that you have been asked to write a school essay on this topic:

A Friend I Would Like to See Again

1. List several special qualities of this friend.

_____

2. Name a place where you and this friend often went.

_____

3. What caused your separation from this friend?

_____

4. How was this friend different from other friends you have had?

_____

5. How might you make arrangements to see this friend again?

_____

6. What was one memorable experience that you and your friend had together?

_____

If you had developed each of these topics into a paragraph, you might have used these organizational patterns: order of importance, spatial order, cause/effect, comparison/contrast, problem/solution, and chronological order.

Using Narration

Although organizational patterns are determined by the meaning, some patterns are easier to read than others. Which of the following passages do you find easier to read? Circle the number.

Passage #1

One very hot summer day a lion and a wild boar came to the same pond at the same time to get a drink. They fought fiercely over which of them should get to drink first. Suddenly they noticed some vultures flying overhead. They quickly ended their quarrel, deciding that it was better for them to be friends than food for vultures.

Passage #2

A lion and a wild boar decided to be friends when they noticed some vultures flying overhead waiting to use them for food if they continued their fierce quarrel. Their quarrel occurred when they came to the same pond at the same time to get a drink. It was a very hot summer day, and each had insisted on getting to drink first.

You probably found the first passage easier to read, not because the content was different, but because the sequence was different. The first passage tells a story—or narrative—in chronological order. Because narratives are familiar to readers—they have heard stories from the time they were very young children—they are easier to read. On the lines below, put the actions in the order they occur in each passage.

Passage #1	**Passage #2**
fought fiercely	quarrel occurred
noticed some vultures	came to the same pond
came to the pond	noticed some vultures
ended their quarrel	decided to be friends

1._____   1._____

2._____   2._____

3._____   3._____

4._____   4._____

Although you cannot write everything in a narrative form, you can often include narrative sentences or groups of sentences in other types of writing.

Recognizing Choices

In the passages below, notice that the same topic generates very different content when the organizational pattern changes. See whether you can match the passage with the organizational pattern. On the line below each passage, tell how you might include a narrative passage in an essay developing this topic. (For the passage you identify as chronological order, leave the line blank.) The first one has been done for you.

- comparison/contrast
- problem/solution
- spatial order

- chronological order
- order of importance
- cause/effect

Topic: Canoeing on the Fox River

1. Our favorite picnic spot on the Fox River is a small clearing where majestic yellow sandstone bluffs line the east and west sides of the river. To the south is a small island jungle, centered in the middle of the river, with narrow water pathways on either side. To the north, far in the distance, we can see the tops of prairie grass.

    Organizational pattern: _____*Spatial Order*_____

    The writer could tell about a particular picnic experience at this spot.

2. As we pushed our canoes off the bank of the Fox River, we saw that the current was running more swiftly than usual. Joe told us not to worry. "Just keep your canoes going with the current, not across it," he said. For several hours, we rode along enjoying the trip and feeling quite certain that our fears were unfounded. Suddenly, just as we were nearing shore for lunch, Joe screamed, "No!"

    Organizational pattern: _____

    _____

3. Dry, hot summers are bad for canoers on the Fox River. Sometimes in July the lack of rain slows the water down to a trickle in some spots. The hot sun evaporates what little water there is left. As a result, canoers find themselves having to portage their boats over one dry patch after another. If they don't, they run the risk of hitting bottom and damaging the canoe.

Organizational pattern: _____

_____

4. In both summer and winter, the Fox River is a vacationer's paradise. Summer weekends bring out hundreds of canoers, who travel along this water highway to enjoy the scenery and the exercise. Although the sun can be intense, the cool breeze from the water and the movement of the canoe keeps boaters comfortable. In the winter, ice skaters take over. Campfires along the banks provide relaxation from hockey and warmth from the penetrating cold.

Organizational pattern: _____

_____

5. As erosion from farm fields fills in the Fox River, canoeing during the summer months is becoming more difficult. Canoers are forced to portage at many shallow spots. The problem could be solved if channels were dredged in these spots. Dirt from the channels could be returned to the fields or used to build up low spots, helping both the farmers and the canoers.

Organizational pattern: _____

_____

6. The Fox River is the perfect place for the beginner in canoeing. Even in the spring, it is shallow enough to be relatively safe. Rental canoes are readily available for a modest price from several companies along the river. Most important, the exercise and lush scenery make it healthy for mind and body.

Organizational pattern: _____

_____

Making Choices

Recall a favorite toy (or collection) that you had when you were a child. In the lines below, describe what you might include in an essay or story about this toy if you developed it using each of the different patterns listed below.

Topic: My Favorite Childhood Toy

(Chronological Order) _____

_____

_____

(Spatial) _____

_____

_____

(Comparison/Contrast) _____

_____

_____

(Problem/Solution) _____

_____

_____

(Order of Importance) _____

_____

_____

(Cause/Effect) _____

_____

_____

*Answers, p. 55-56: 2. Chronological 3. Cause/effect 4. Comparison/contrast 5. Problem/solution 6. Importance

Think of some store that you went to frequently when you were little. What did it look like inside and out? What kinds of things were in this store? Do you recall buying anything or wanting to buy things? Do you remember the store clerk? Was this store a favorite? What emotions does thinking about this store create in you? Write an essay or story about this store, using one of the following overall patterns. Use narration whenever appropriate.

- comparison/contrast
- problem/solution
- spatial order

- chronological order
- order of importance
- cause/effect

_____

_____

_____

_____

_____

_____

_____

_____

_____

_____

_____

_____

_____

Share your story or essay with the class.

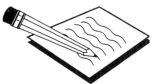

CHAPTER 4
Making Ideas Clear and Concise

Letting Verbs Be Verbs

Understanding Choices

Verbs are action words, right?

Of course they are, but they are used many other ways, too. Here are some examples of verbs showing action. Write the action verbs in the blanks on the right.

1. A dachshund scampers noisily across the hall. _____

2. The storm clouds moved quickly. _____

3. The forward shoots for three points and the team moves to first. _____

Verbs also show state of being or linking. Write the verbs in the blanks on the right.

1. Sarah seems sad today. _____

2. The turkey smells delicious. _____

3. A pizza sounds great. _____

Verbs can also be helpers to indicate time and duration. Write the helping verbs in the blanks.

1. In one more year, I will take a test for my driving permit. _____

2. Did your family travel to Quebec and Nova Scotia last year? _____

3. You have been working on that term project for a month! _____

Verbs can be used as nouns and adjectives. Notice how the "ing" words below are used as subjects and modifiers, even though they are also familiar verbs. Write them in the blanks.

1. Running keeps me in shape. _____

2. The running water in the creek was a sign of spring. _____

3. The hunter held a smoking gun. _____

Recognizing Choices

Using verbs to show action.

If action is what you are emphasizing, then it is an action verb you need to use. Sometimes writers use nouns when they really intend to show the action of a verb. For example, in the following sentences, the verb *study* is important to the meaning. Circle the sentence that best expresses this action.

A. We **did a study** of polite expressions used in Spanish.

B. We **studied** polite expressions used in Spanish.

If you chose sentence B, you chose the active verb. If you chose sentence A, you chose a verb together with a noun to express the same meaning. Most of the time, an active verb expresses the meaning more effectively. Make a habit of using verbs rather than nouns to express actions.

Here is another example. Rewrite the following sentence, using the verb *retracted* instead of *made a retraction of*.

The newspaper ~~made a retraction of~~ the statement about the mayor's spending.

_____

In the sentence above, the expression *made a retraction* includes the following verb and noun:

the verb *made* + the noun *retraction*

A stronger expression of the meaning in this sentence is achieved by using the verb *retracted* instead.

The newspaper retracted the statement about the mayor's spending.

Below are some familiar nouns. Fill in the chart with the verbs that could be used to express the action suggested by these nouns. The first one is done for you.

Noun Form	Verb Form
intention	intend
reaction	
refusal	
discovery	
discussion	
accomplishment	
location	
dream	

Write the following sentences according to the directions below and then decide whether the noun or the verb states the action more effectively.

1. A. Write a sentence using the phrase *made a discovery*.

   _____

   B. Now rewrite your sentence using the verb *discovered* instead of *made a discovery*.

   _____

2. A. Write a sentence using the phrase *found the location of*.

   _____

   B. Now rewrite your sentence using the verb *located* instead of *found the location of*.

   _____

Making Choices

Practice using active verbs. Rewrite the following sentences by replacing the italicized noun with its verb form. The first one is done for you.

1. A *correction* in the amount of the gratuity added to the bill was made by the waiter.

   The waiter corrected the amount of the gratuity added to the bill.

2. Today there will be an *inspection* by the engineers of the new school building site.

   _____

   _____

3. Joe made a *plan* to celebrate his birthday by renting a disco and hiring a good DJ.

   _____

   _____

4. There was a *recommendation* from the computer club that the school add five Internet sites.

   _____

   _____

5. Ann had an *intention* to accept all the responsibilities of club president.

   _____

   _____

6. Ted had a *dream* of reaching his goal to snow-board the half-pipe.

   _____

   _____

Avoiding Wordiness

Understanding Choices

Knowing when to use repetition.

Repetition is not necessarily bad. Sometimes it is very good. Repetition is used effectively by many writers. However, when repetition is "wordy" or "redundant," then it is not good because the writer says more than is needed and the wordiness actually detracts from the writing.

The following excerpts from a work by a famous American writer show the power of repetition when it is used for emphasis. (Can you name the writer and the story from which these excerpts are taken?)

_____

"She had a little thin face and a little thin body, thin light hair, and a sour expression."

1. What words are repeated? _____

2. What is the writer emphasizing through the use of repetition? _____

_____

Here is the second excerpt. (Did you guess the writer and the story yet?)

"So when she was a sickly, fretful, ugly little baby, she was kept out of the way, and when she became a sickly, fretful, toddling thing, she was kept out of the way."

1. What is repeated? _____

2. What is the writer emphasizing through the use of repetition? _____

_____

(Did you guess *The Secret Garden* by Frances Hodgson Burnett?)

Recognizing Choices

Knowing when repetition is "wordiness."
Even through repetition can be used very effectively, sometimes writers are repetitious in a negative way. This kind of repetition is usually referred to as wordiness: for example, when expressions are used that do not really add anything at all, when the writer uses many words to express what could have been said in a word or two, or when the writer makes too many comments about his or her own writing.

Read the following passage and underline the words and phrases that make this passage wordy.

> When all is said and done, Mark Twain's novel *The Adventures of Huckleberry Finn* is a story of a boy and a man who travel up the Mississippi River. Their experiences teach them many lessons about human nature. First and foremost, they meet many different types of people, some who are admirable and others who are despicable. I think that this story teaches readers to be tolerant and to trust their own personal values. Huck does not trust his own values at first. He goes against them when he rescues Jim from slavery. Huck even thinks he will go to hell for this crime since Jim is someone's property. In the final outcome, Huck reflects back on his crime and decides that he was right to free Jim and that he would do it over again. Huck learns to believe in himself and trust his own instincts. Any and all readers will find in this book a valuable theme that applies each and every day.

Now list below the wordy expressions you have underlined in the above passage. Then replace them with more concise expressions or write *omit* if the words should be left out altogether.

Wordy Expression	Concise Expression (or Omit)

Cross out the repetition in the following sentences:

1. The boss said he wanted a full and complete report.

2. The test is scheduled for 2:00 p.m. on Tuesday afternoon.

3. The red colored jacket was visible to the eye from a block away.

4. During the tornado drill, all students are to assemble together in the downstairs hall.

5. The hot air balloon ascended upward very slowly and left a faint vapor trail.

6. To reach the post office, you must proceed forward on Main Street for two more blocks.

7. Each and every student is participating in the science contest.

8. Every individual team member's effort is important to the team's success.

9. At the store's grand opening, each tenth customer was presented a free gift.

10. The photo album brought back many past memories.

Making Choices

The following paragraph is "wordy." Edit this paragraph by crossing out the unnecessary words and phrases. Then rewrite a concise version below.

FIRE EMERGENCY DRILL PROCEDURE FOR ROOM #25

In the event of a fire alarm emergency warning signal, all students present at school should immediately move calmly and quietly out of the room. They should proceed forward down the west staircase individually and in single file, one behind the other. It is necessary that all students then completely exit the building through the west door at the bottom of the stairway. Each and every person must proceed across the street to the other side, where they should wait for further instructions.

_____

_____

_____

_____

_____

_____

_____

_____

_____

_____

_____

_____

Choosing the Right Word

Understanding Choices

What is the right word?

The right word depends on audience, purpose, and occasion. For example, if you are describing the new YMCA in your neighborhood to your friends, you might say "it's rockin'," and they would understand you completely. However, if you were trying to convince your parents to buy a membership, you might describe it as "a good deal." If you were talking to the YMCA manager about getting a summer job, you might describe the Y as "a wonderful opportunity." The right word usually depends on audience, your purpose, and the occasion.

If you think about it, you already know if you are being too formal with your friends or too informal with adults or strangers. And if you have studied foreign languages, you know that most languages other than English have both an informal word for *you* and a formal word for *you*. For example, in French, one always uses "vous" (the formal word for "you") when speaking to an acquaintance or stranger. The French word "tu" (the informal word for "you") is reserved for family members and close friends.

Imagine that you are waiting at the corner for your bus. The following people come by as you are waiting. How do you greet each of them? Use their names and a greeting appropriate for each individual.

(your younger brother) _____

(your teacher) _____

(your mom) _____

(your best friend) _____

(your mom's or dad's business associate) _____

(the mayor) _____

(your aunt or uncle)_____

(your bus driver) _____

Recognizing Choices

Sometimes student writers try to impress their readers by using vocabulary that is too formal for the occasion. This is pompous diction. Read the following paragraph and circle the words that you think are pompous (puffed up or inflated).

To: Art Club Members
From: Art Club President
Re: Next Meeting

The art club will convene for its first regularly scheduled meeting at 4:30 p.m. in the afternoon on the twenty-third day of September. Members are requested to assemble in the northwest quadrant of the cafeteria premises. The meeting will commence at 3:30 p.m. and last for a duration of approximately one hour. The business to be conducted will be two-fold: the election of officers and a paradigm for future meetings. All members should arrive expeditiously.

Write the circled words or phrases below in the first column. Write a better choice of wording for this audience and occasion in the second column.

Pompous Word Choices	Better Word Choices for the Audience and Occasion

Sometimes young people get so accustomed to speaking in the slang they use with their friends that they use it when they are speaking to teachers, employers, other adult professionals, and acquaintances of the family. Read the following paragraph and circle the words that you think are too informal for such an audience and occasion.

To: Superintendent of Schools
From: The Art Club
Re: Art Fair

   The dudes in the art club have come up with a rockin' idea for holding an art fair at our school. There are three awesome reasons why an art fair would be good for SHS. First of all, art fairs are hot—kids really like a chance to show off their sketches, drawings, paintings, sculptures, and other creative stuff. Second, an art fair at our school would mean big bucks for the art club because all the dudes from the other schools would be chowing down and we would get the bread for the concessions. Last, the art fair would be a really cool way to get more dudes to join the art club. We hope you'll give us a thumbs up on this request.

Now write those words and expressions that you circled in the first column. In the second column write the words that you think would be better choices for this audience and occasion.

Slang Expressions	Better Word Choices for the Audience and Occasion

Making Choices

Imagine that the boxes below are notepad pages. Write a message to each of the three audiences telling them you will be late for your meeting with them (you decide the kind of meeting). Use the words that you would usually use with your best friend, your mom and dad, and your teacher. Notice how your word choice changes when the audience changes.

Writing in the Positive

Understanding Choices

Know when to use *not*.

The word *not* is a powerful word in our language, but you should not overuse it in your writing—use it sparingly and use it when it is most effective. One of the greatest values of the word *not* is in statements where it expresses "antithesis," which means pairing up two opposite items to create a dramatic contrast. For example, in the play *Julius Caesar*, Shakespeare uses antithesis in the following lines spoken by Brutus, a character who disapproves of Caesar but must speak at Caesar's funeral. Notice how the word *not* helps to pair up opposite attitudes.

"I come not to praise Caesar, but to bury Caesar."

Shakespeare also uses antithesis in Hamlet's famous line:

"To be or not to be; that is the question."

Other examples of antithesis include the following:

If you are not part of the solution, you are part of the problem.

Don't be square; be there.

Think of examples of antithesis you have heard, or make up your own and write them below. (Do you know a famous example of antithesis from John F. Kennedy's "Inaugural Address"?)

_____

_____

_____

_____

Know when to avoid using *not*.

As a general rule, good writers avoid using *not* when an idea could be expressed just as well or better in a positive statement. For example, "Do not be late" in the positive is "Be on time." Since readers can understand positive statements more easily than negative statements, the word *not* in some situations may actually cloud the meaning of an idea rather than clarify it. Look at the following sentences. On the blanks below, finish rewriting each sentence without *not* and then consider which statement is clearer.

Katie did not think that learning keyboarding skills was unimportant.

Katie thought that _____.

Joe did not think that learning keyboarding skills was important.

Joe thought that _____.

Recognizing Choices

Now read each of the pairs of sentences below and decide which you think is the clearer statement. Circle the one you think is better.

1. a. John is not old enough yet to get his driver's license.
   b. John is too young to get his driver's license.

2. a. Sarah passed the class.
   b. Sarah did not receive a failing grade in the class.

3. a. Do not use the negative.
   b. Use the affirmative.

4. a. Do not come home after your 10 p.m. curfew.
   b. Come home before your 10 p.m. curfew.

5. a. Shane thought Adam left before the party ended.
   b. Shane thought Adam had not stayed at the party until it ended.

For each of the following negative expressions in the first box, write a positive expression in the second box that expresses the same idea. The first one is done for you.

Negative	Positive
not certain	uncertain
not ever	
not happy	
not predictable	
not absent	
not well	
not expected	
not forgotten	
not believable	

Get into the habit of writing in the positive. Rewrite the following phrases as positives. A suggestion is given for the first one.

1. Ann is *not certain* about the cost of the new computer system. (Use *uncertain*.)

_____.

2. Jane's parents suspected that she was *not being honest* with them.

_____.

3. Tim *didn't trust* the rumors he had heard; the source was not honest.

_____.

4. The data was *not complete*; furthermore, the calculations did not seem accurate.

_____.

5. Technology is always changing; therefore, we *cannot expect not to need retraining*.

_____.

Answers, page 72: Katie thought that learning keyboarding skills was important. Joe thought that learning keyboarding skills was unimportant. 1. B, 2. A, 3. B, 4. B, 5. A

Making Choices

In the space below, write a letter to parents in which you discuss the amount of freedom that you think parents should give their middle-school-aged children. Make your meaning clear by using the positive throughout most of your letter. Also, see if you can include one example of antithesis.

Dear Parents:

_____

_____

_____

_____

_____

_____

_____

Sincerely,

_____

Softening Bad News

Understanding Choices

Do you ever wonder how letters with bad news can sound so good? To accomplish this result, workplace writers use a strategy called *burying the bad news.* This strategy involves making choices about how to deliver bad news so the overall tone of the letter will be positive—in spite of the fact that the news will not please the reader.

Burying bad news is not a new strategy, and it is not even unique to writing. This technique is based on the same principle expressed in a popular song from the Disney movie *Mary Poppins*, "Just a spoon full of sugar makes the medicine go down." It is a principle that is also used humorously in the familiar joke beginning, "I've got some good news and some bad news." Burying bad news by mixing it with good news makes the bitter part more tolerable.

Think of situations in which writers might have to deliver bad news. Explain the situations below.

1. _____

   _____

   _____

2. _____

   _____

   _____

Recognizing Choices

The following letter demonstrates three important steps in delivering bad news. As you read, look for the three important steps listed below. Identify each step by marking **A**, **B**, and **C** on the letter where each step is accomplished. Underline the words that accomplish that step.

A. Position the good news first.
B. Offer a brief apology.
C. Conclude on a positive note.

Bussa Studios
Box 344
Fulton, Indiana 34856

November 20, 1999

Mr. John Howard
322 Weber Street
Medina, Wisconsin 44897

Dear Mr. Howard:

We are pleased to offer you a new sitting at your convenience, free of charge, and we apologize for the defective photographs you received from our studios.

Our labs process thousands of pictures each week, and, although we inspect each order carefully, occasionally, a customer receives a defective product.

We value your business and look forward to serving you in the future. I will call you next week to schedule your new appointment.

Sincerely,

G.B. Ingram

In each of the circumstances below, there is bad news to be delivered. Read the bad news and then fill in the blanks below with the information requested. The first one is done for you.

A) New Honda dirt bike with defective brakes

Who will deliver the bad news? _President of the Honda Corporation_

Who will receive the bad new? _People who have purchased a Honda dirt bike_

How will the news be delivered? _A letter from the company president_

B) Middle school student failing social studies

Who will deliver the bad news? _____

Who will receive the bad news? _____

How will the news be delivered? _____

C) Family's trip canceled due to an airline strike

Who will deliver the bad news? _____

Who will receive the bad news? _____

How will the news be delivered? _____

D) Layoff at a printing company

Who will deliver the bad news? _____

Who will receive the bad news? _____

How will the news be delivered? _____

In each of the following cases, consider what you would say if you were the person who had to deliver the bad news. Write below some good news you could offer first in a letter to help balance the bad news in each case.

A) New Honda dirt bike with defective brakes

_____

_____

B) Middle school student failing social studies

_____

_____

C) Family's trip canceled due to an airline strike

_____

_____

D) Layoff at a printing company

_____

_____

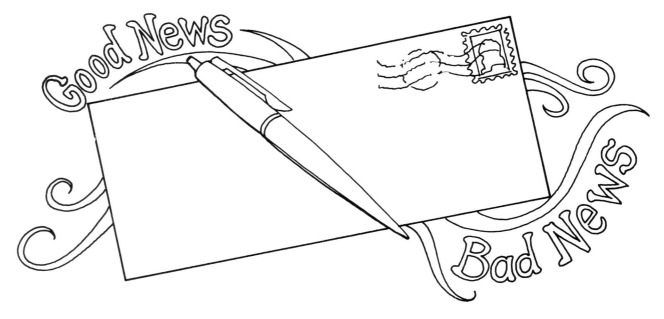

Making Choices

Each of the following scenarios involves bad news that must be delivered. The occasion and the audience is different in each case, but the writer's goal is the same—to bury the bad news. Write a letter for each of the following circumstances. Remember to offer some good new first, then make a brief apology, and, finally, conclude on a positive note.

Bad News Scenario #1: You work in the customer service department for Kodak. You have received a letter from an unhappy consumer who bought three rolls of film for her daughter's class trip to Disney World. The film was defective and none of the students' pictures turned out. You must write a letter responding to the bad news. (Use the sample letter format on page 76.)

Name _____

Bad News Scenario # 2: You are a middle-school math teacher. One of your students is failing badly. It is half-way through the grading period, and you must send a progress report to the parents of this student to let them know the bad news.

Using Introductory Tags

Understanding Choices

Who Says So?
Whether you are writing a story or a report, you must let the reader know who says what. Introductory tags, which are phrases that identify a speaker or a source of information, appear in different forms throughout all writing. For example, typical introductory tags in storytelling are "he said," "she said," and "I said." In report writing, a common introductory tag is the phrase, "According to . . . ." This phrase is used to introduce the name of the author whose information you used in your report. In your writing, you need to make choices about how to introduce the speaker or the source. Be certain that you make choices that serve the reader, so your reader will understand not only what is being said but also "Who says so."

Recognizing Choices

In Narratives: Stories, novels, biographies, and other narratives usually contain conversation between characters called dialogue. When you first learned how to read, you probably noticed that, along with those familiar introductory tags such as "I (he, she, etc.) said," quotation marks and a new paragraph also signal a new speaker. For example, notice the signals in the following lines of quotation from Mary Shelley's novel *Frankenstein*. In this part of the story, after several years' separation, Dr. Frankenstein again confronts the monster he had created. The doctor, who is also the narrator, is enraged by news that his monster has murdered an innocent child. As you read the lines below, circle the tags used to signal who says what (notice that some lines do not have tags). Then indicate who is speaking, the monster or Dr. Frankenstein. The first one is done for you.

1. "Devil," I exclaimed, "do you dare approach me?" . . .   _____Dr. Frankenstein_____

2. "I expected this reception," said the demon . . .   _____

3. "Abhorred monster! Fiend . . . ! The tortures of hell are too mild a vengeance for thy crimes." My rage was without bounds; I sprang on him . . .   _____

4. He easily eluded me and said, "Be calm! I entreat you to hear me . . ."   _____

5. "Be gone! I will not hear you . . . we are enemies." . . .   _____

6. "How can I move thee? Will no entreaties cause thee to turn a favourable eye upon thy creature . . . ?"   _____

Tags or No Tags?

Authors do not always use tags in each line. In some cases, other signals—the content, the quotation marks, the dialect, and the new paragraph—are sufficient to tell the reader who is speaking. As a writer, you have a choice; you may use tags in some cases and not in others. Whatever your choice, be certain to give your reader clear signals as to who is speaking.

As you read the following excerpt from *Huckleberry Finn* by Mark Twain, notice that there are no tags. In this passage, Huckleberry and his simple-minded friend, Jim, are traveling down the Mississippi River on a raft. During a heavy fog, the two are separated for awhile. Jim thinks Huck has drowned, and Huck decides to play a mean trick on Jim by pretending the whole incident is just Jim's imagination. As you read the passage, see if the author's other signals, without the use of tags, are sufficient clues as to who is speaking. Write the name of the speaker in each blank below. The first one is done for you.

1. "Hello, Jim, have I been asleep? Why didn't you stir me up?"   _____Huck_____

2. "Goodness gracious, is dat you, Huck? En you ain' dead— you ain' drownded—you's back agin? It's too good for true. . ." _____

3. "What's the matter with you, Jim? You been a-drinking?" _____

4. "Drinkin? Has I ben a-drinkin? Has I had a chance to be a-drinkin?" _____

5. "Well, then, what makes you talk so wild?" _____

6. "How does I talk wild?" _____

7. "How? Why, hain't you been talking about my coming back, and all that stuff, as if I'd been gone away?" _____

8. "Huck—Huck Finn, you look me in de eye; . . . Hain't you ben gone away?" _____

9. "Gone away? Why, what in the nation do you mean? . . . Where would I go to?" _____

10. "Well, looky here, boss, dey's sumfn wrong, dey is. Is I *me*, or who *is* I? Is I heah, or whah is I? Now dat's what I wants to know." _____

11. "Well, I think you're here, plain enough, but I think you're a tangle-headed old fool, Jim." _____

Answers to page 81: 2. said the demon, the demon; 3. no tag, Dr. Frankenstein; 4. He . . . said, the demon; 5. no tag, Dr. Frankenstein; 6. no tag, the demon

In Reports: Introductory tags are also important in report writing. For example, in the following excerpt from a student report on soldiers and weapons of the future, the writer uses the introductory tag, "According to Jane Mason," in order to let the reader know the original source of the report's information on future warfare. Notice that this paragraph is not a direct quotation; rather, it is a paraphrase of a passage from a magazine article. In either case, whether paraphrase or direct quotation, the writer must use a tag to identify and introduce borrowed information. The number in parenthesis is the page number on which the information appears in the article.

Read the following paragraphs and then answer the questions below each excerpt.

According to Jane Mason, author of "No Soldiers," in fifty years the United States will use robotic soldiers, which will be able to greatly outperform human soldiers. These robots will be able to walk hundreds of miles a day and lift hundreds of pounds (10).

1. What is the introductory tag? _____

2. Who is the original source of this information?_____

3. On what page of the original article would this information be found? _____

In another example from a student report called "Future Couch Potatoes," the student writer uses a direct quotation. Again, as with the paraphrase, the writer must use a tag to introduce borrowed information.

In the future, we won't have to get off the couch at all. We will shop from home by computer. Electronic bulletin boards on our TV/computer units will replace newspaper classifieds. We'll order pizza on-line and party with our friends via on-line video connections. Author John Donaldson says we will even be able to "jump in on our favorite TV programs through interactive soaps and make virtual visits to our friends' homes" (20).

1. What is the introductory tag? _____

2. Who is the original source of this information?_____

3. On what page of the original article would this information be found? _____

Answers, page 82: 2. Jim, 3. Huck, 4. Jim, 5. Huck, 6. Jim, 7. Huck, 8. Jim, 9. Huck, 10. Jim, 11. Huck

Making Choices

In Narratives: Imagine the future! Assume that you and your friends had an on-line video party. Below write a narrative about the party, which includes dialogue among you and your friends. Remember to use quotation marks around each speaker's words and change paragraphs every time the speaker changes. Use tags where necessary. In places where the speaker is apparent through other signals, leave out the tags. Be certain that your readers get clear signals as to who is speaking.

In Essays: Report on the future! Read an article on future cars, homes, fashion, or lifestyles. Then write a report on that information, paraphrasing the information from your source. Begin with an introductory tag to name the source of your information. Add the page number of your source in parenthesis at the end.

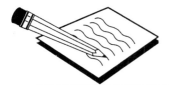

CHAPTER 5
Creating Your Own Style
Using Sentence Variety

Understanding Choices

Even if each of your sentences is technically flawless, your writing may still lack interest. In addition to having your writing appropriate for your audience and purpose, you want your writing to reflect you—your personality and your style. To do this you can personalize your writing and make it more interesting by using sentence variety, figures of speech, headings, and even visual information.

Sentence Types

There are many different types of sentences. The more types you know, the more choices you will have available.

Declarative. A declarative sentence makes a statement.

　　Example: Mark ran a mile.

Interrogative. An interrogative sentence asks a question.

　　Example: Is he the fastest runner in the school?

Imperative. An imperative sentence gives a command or makes a request.

　　Example: Cheer for Mark as he crosses the finish line.

Exclamatory. An exclamatory sentence shows strong feeling.

　　Example: Wow! That was a great race to win, Mark!

(Note: Occasionally sentence fragments are quite effective. Example: What a runner!)

Write a declarative sentence below. Then rewrite it as each of the other sentence types. Notice that when you change types, you also change the order of words.

Declarative _____

Interrogative _____

Imperative _____

Exclamatory _____

Sentence Length

Short, simple sentences are quite effective. They add variety to your writing and they create emphasis, especially when they are surrounded by several long sentences. It is the contrast that makes them interesting. Notice the contrasting lengths of the sentences in the following paragraph.

He was bent over at the waist, his gnarly hand resting on a wooden cane that shook ever so slightly, his shoulders stooped, and his thinning, gray hair falling into his eyes as though every strand joined in the effort to propel him down the hallway. His breathing was shallow but rapid, every footstep causing him to gasp for more air, air that smelled of the disinfectant the nursing home used without fail. He was old. As he rounded the corner and navigated into the recreation room, a smile appeared on his face because he saw that his three friends who loved to play cards were already seated and waiting for their weekly game of bridge.

1. Underline the short sentence. Add another short sentence that will bring the paragraph to a powerful end.
   Write it here: _____

Because you will want to make your writing interesting, you will need to use a variety of short *and* long sentences. Too many short sentences make writing choppy. On the other hand, too many long sentences may confuse the reader.

2. Create a paragraph of your own by writing two long sentences followed by one short sentence.

_____

_____

_____

_____

_____

_____

_____

_____

_____

_____

Sentence Structures

Sentence structures include the various ways words are arranged or ordered in a sentence. Sometimes certain arrangements are used regularly enough that they create a pattern. Knowing these patterns and what they can add to your writing will help you to achieve clarity, power, and style.

Repetition of words, phrases, clauses, and even sentences can be very effective and can help your audience to understand your ideas. For example, most of us remember the refrain of a song even if we do not remember the rest of the words.

1. The *Gettysburg Address* uses repetition to advantage. Fill in the repeated words.

   A. We cannot dedicate—_____ _____ consecrate—

   _____ _____ hallow—this ground.

   B. . . . and that government of _____ _____, by _____

   _____, and for _____ _____, shall not

   perish from the earth.

When repetition is removed, notice what happens to the above sentences: "We cannot dedicate, consecrate, or hallow this ground. . . . government of, by, and for the people, shall not perish from the earth." In some cases, especially when you desire to emphasize certain words or phrases, you may choose to repeat a word or phrase as was done in *The Gettysburg Address.* In other cases, when you desire to keep your message short and to the point, you may choose to omit repetition.

2. Think of audiences and purposes when you would want to use repetition. Think of audiences and purposes when you would not want to use repetition. Write Y if you would use repetition and N if you would not use repetition in the following instances. Explain your response.

   _____   A. A persuasive speech urging coaches to buy your brand of uniforms

   _____   B. A letter to a dissatisfied customer saying that your company will refund her money for the computer she recently purchased but did not meet her standards

   _____   C. A brochure urging teenagers to drive defensively

Sometimes repetition involves repeating the key word once. Notice the difference between the following sentences.

If I had a friend who would truly understand me, I'd be happy.
If I had a friend, a friend who would truly understand me, I'd be happy.

Although the first sentence is clear, in some cases the second sentence may be more powerful.

3. In the following sentence fill in the blank by repeating the key word from the preceding phrase.

A. A gift of money, _____ to buy baseball cards, new clothes, and the latest video, would make Jeremy happy.

B. Being busy freshmen, Pam and Joe needed time, _____ to finish the homecoming float, to decorate the gym, and to buy refreshments for the dance.

C. On the lines below write a sentence of your own which follows the same pattern.

_____

_____

Sometimes you may wish to obtain the effect that repetition achieves without repeating the exact words. You can achieve the same effect of repetition by using parallel words or phrases. You may repeat the same part of speech or the same type of phrase. For example, if you would like to list three favorite pastimes of middle school students in a sentence, you can achieve your goal by using the same types of words or phrases: Middle school students enjoyed *visiting, dancing,* and *bowling* at the activity night.

4. Read the following sentences. Fill in the blank with a word or phrase that is the same part of speech as the first word in the series.

A. At Northgate Middle School, students love to surf the Internet, to watch old movies, and _____.

B. Jared's neighbor walked down the street slowly, carefully, and _____.

C. On the lines below, write a sentence of your own which follows the same pattern.

_____

_____

Answers to page 87: 2. A. Y, B. N, C. Y

Recognizing Choices

The following activities ask you to study repetition and its effects. Select one (or, even better, all) of them to complete.

1. Effective use of repetition appears in *The Declaration of Independence*. Because the same beginning words are used, the grievances against King George are emphasized: "He has refused . . . He has forbidden . . . He has dissolved . . . He has obstructed . . . " This is a partial list. Examine this historical document and continue this list. How does repetition help to make this message appropriate to the audience and purpose?

2. Read the first sentence of Charles Dickens' *A Tale of Two Cities*. List the repetitive clauses. What makes them effective?

3. Read the first sentence of *The Outsiders* by S. E. Hinton. Then read the last sentence of the book. What do you notice? How can this type of repetition be effective?

The following activities ask you to consider sentence variety. Read the following paragraph from *A Christmas Carol* by Charles Dickens.

> Scrooge knew he was dead? Of course he did. How could it be otherwise? Scrooge and he were partners for I don't know how many years. Scrooge was his sole executor, his sole administrator, his sole assign, his sole residuary legatee, his sole friend, and sole mourner. And even Scrooge was not so dreadfully cut up by the sad event, but that he was an excellent man of business on the very day of the funeral, and solemnised it with an undoubted bargain.

4. Write your own paragraph below, using the sentence patterns that Dickens has used, describing a person you know. The first sentences are started for you.

_____ knew _____ was _____? Of course

_____ did! How could it be otherwise? _____

_____

_____

_____

Making Choices

Carefully read Martin Luther King, Jr.'s "I Have a Dream" speech. Examine the types of sentences and the lengths of sentences King used in his speech. Then look at the repetition that appears in the speech. In small groups, discuss these stylistic devices. How do they contribute to the clarity, power, and style of the speech?

Like King, you may have a dream, a dream for yourself or for your country. Write your own "I Have a Dream" speech using repetition. Try to create an original phrase, a phrase that has special significance to you. Also pay attention to sentence types and length as you write and revise your speech. Write the final draft of your speech on this page.

_____

_____

_____

_____

_____

_____

_____

_____

_____

_____

_____

_____

_____

_____

_____

_____

Using Figures of Speech

Understanding Choices

You have probably noticed that no two writers write exactly the same way. Their writing reflects personal preferences, or choices, and these choices have shaped their particular writing styles. In fact, some writers have such distinctive styles that their works are easily identifiable.

As you continue to develop your own writing style, you may choose to use figures of speech in some of your writing. Once again, your choice of whether to use them will depend on your audience and purpose. Figures of speech describe one thing in terms of another thing. For instance, when Shakespeare has Romeo exclaim, "Juliet is the sun," he is describing Juliet in terms of the brightness and warmth of the sun. In this way, figures of speech go beyond stating the dictionary meaning of a word. Because they do not mean literally what the writer says, they require that the reader expand literal thinking to imaginative thinking. The most common figures of speech are *simile, metaphor*, and *personification*.

Similes

Similes compare two unlike objects using the words *like* or *as*. Because similes use the words *like* or *as*, they are fairly easy to spot in writing. The following sentence includes a simile: "The freshly plowed fields are like yards of corduroy." You can probably immediately picture the plowed furrows of soft earth which are like the soft lines in corduroy fabric.

A good simile is original. Try to create similes that will stimulate your readers' imagination. Complete each sentence below, creating a simile from the following list— or better yet, create your own. Share your similes and explain the connections.

My hair looks like a(n)_____	snail sand
Time is like _____	tornado food
Computers are as _____ as _____	jungle tiger
Middle school is like _____	hornet scout
	birds' nest lightning
John was as angry as a(n) _____	gold cat
Heather stepped as softly as a(n) _____	good necessary

Metaphors

Although metaphors also compare two unlike objects, they are less obvious than similes. Metaphors do not contain words, such as *like* or *as*, that signal the comparison; the comparison is more direct—one thing *becomes* another. The following sentence is an example of a metaphor: "Jeremy's mind was a kaleidoscope of thoughts." In this case, Jeremy's mind becomes a kaleidoscope, an ever-changing mix of colorful and creative ideas.

While metaphors often appear in poetry, you may also choose to use them in prose. A famous metaphor appears in the short poem "Fog" by Carl Sandburg. In this poem, fog becomes a cat.

In what ways are fog and a cat similar? _____

A common metaphorical expression often occurs in prose when government is referred to as a machine.

In what ways are government and a machine similar?_____

_____

Although metaphors compare two things that are normally not compared, the two objects cannot be too similar (such as the sun and a yellow-orange ball). Yet there must exist some thread of similarity. What is the similarity between the two words in each of the following pairs? Place an X in the blank if the two words are so similar that they cannot be metaphorical.

road	ribbon	_____
friendship	seed	_____
story	tapestry	_____
soil	field	_____
life	candle	_____
memories	jewels	_____
cloud	cotton	_____

Extended Metaphor

Sometimes a writer will continue the metaphorical comparison for more than one sentence. In this case, the comparison continues throughout several passages or stanzas, sometimes the entire work. "O Captain! My Captain" by Walt Whitman is an example of an extended metaphor. Whitman extends the metaphor of Abraham Lincoln being the captain of a ship (the country) throughout the poem. Read this poem. Discuss the ways that the metaphor of a ship is extended.

Create your own extended metaphor by completing the following four steps.
1. Choose your own subject. (Example: best friend)
2. Select a metaphor for your subject. (Example: diamond)
3. Think of three characteristics of the metaphor you chose in #2. (Example: best friends have many facets, best friends sparkle, best friends are priceless)
4. Write one or more sentences (or stanzas) for each trait to create your extended metaphor.

Idioms

Sometimes metaphors have been used so frequently that they have become a part of our everyday speech. These expressions are so peculiar to our language that they cannot be easily translated into another language. Such metaphorical expressions are called *idioms*. Because idioms cannot be translated literally, non-native speakers often experience difficulty understanding them. Below are a few of the thousands of idioms that we take for granted and use every day. Explain what each of the following idioms means.

Some idioms involve direction:
What's up?
The joke went right over Pam's head.
Joe has something up his sleeve.
Polly went out on a limb to help Joey.

Other idioms involve parts of the human body:
Keep a stiff upper lip.
Get off my back.
He has a chip on his shoulder.

Many idiomatic expressions find their origins in sports:
Give me a ballpark figure.
You're out in left field.
The salesman plays hard ball.
Be certain to cover your bases.
She's out of his league.

You probably had no trouble understanding the above sentences. However, as a writer, you will want to choose when to use such expressions. While they add color to writing, they are also often typical of informal writing.

Make a list of idioms you have heard recently. Compare your list with lists of your classmates. Try to place the idiomatic expressions into various groups as was done in the previous examples. You may create a group of idioms which contain animals: "Melissa let the cat out of the bag." Or you may create a group of idioms which contain food: "Rachel is the apple of her father's eye."

List two idioms below.

_____

_____

Personification

Personification does not compare two items in the same way as similes and metaphors compare. Rather, when writers use personification, they give objects (or even ideas) human qualities. These human qualities add a new dimension to the things, a dimension that ordinary description cannot add. "The field of dandelions danced in the breeze," is an example of a sentence which contains personification. Notice that *the field of dandelions* is the thing being described and that *danced* is the human quality given to the field. We do not normally associate dandelions with dancing, but we can imagine how dandelions would look "dancing" in the breeze.

In the chart below fill in the objects and the human qualities that are given to the object.

Sentence	Object	Human Quality
1. Rows of corn stood at attention in the stifling heat of late August.	_____	_____
2. The floor cried out for help under the weight of the machinery.	_____	_____
3. As it caromed off the front of the rim, the basketball laughed at me.	_____	_____
4. The sun smiled upon the flowers.	_____	_____
5. Jealousy gnawed at Lorenzo's stomach for days.	_____	_____

Recognizing Choices

Your choice concerning whether or not to use figurative language depends on your audience and purpose. In creative writing you would use a lot of figurative language. In technical writing you would not.

Fill in the chart with the kind of figurative language you would use in each situation: simile, metaphor, extended metaphor, idiom, or personification. In some situations you may *not* wish to use any kind of figurative language. If that is so, write *none* in the blank. In other cases you may wish to use more than one kind of figurative language.

Audience	Form and Purpose	Figurative Language
middle school students	poem about friendship	_____
teachers	invitation to school play	_____
readers of local newspaper	sports article	_____
fifth graders	story about a bird and a field used to represent life	_____
first graders	poem about the feelings of a teddy bear	_____
parents	letter persuading them of the benefits of a class trip	_____
foreign exchange student	letter welcoming him or her to the school	_____

*Answers to page 94: 1. rows of corn, stood; 2. floor, cried; 3. basketball, laughed; 4. sun, smiled; 5. Jealousy, gnawed

Making Choices

Complete each writing situation, keeping in mind your audience and purpose. Use figurative language wherever you think it is appropriate. Use the back of this sheet if you need more room.

Brochure
Audience: fifth-grade students
Purpose: to explain how to format a disk or load a computer program

_____

_____

_____

Article
Audience: readers of middle school newspaper
Purpose: to report about a tournament championship game in middle school basketball

_____

_____

_____

Story
Audience: kindergarten children
Purpose: to tell about a day your pet went to school

_____

_____

_____

_____

Poem
Audience: adults
Purpose: to share your feelings about your future goals

_____

_____

_____

_____

Share these with your classmates. In which writing situations did you use figurative language? Which kinds of figurative language did you use?

Creating Headings

Understanding Choices

Headings are bold-faced words or phrases that label and divide sections of a piece of writing. Headings can be very useful to both readers and writers. You have seen headings used in your textbooks, in newspapers and magazines, in encyclopedia information, and in most fliers or brochures announcing sales or events. They clearly show the reader where each section begins and ends, and they break up the visual monotony of a text with white space and larger type size. Headings are very helpful to the reader; they create what is referred to as "reader-friendly" text.

Locate two examples of headings used in magazines, newspapers, catalogs, or advertisements. Paste your examples below and label them by writing the source where you found them.

Source: _____   Source: _____

Recognizing Choices

Headings also serve the writer very well by providing an organizational structure to follow. Often the headings of a report correspond to the report's table of contents. When a writer cannot decide on the right heading, that is often a clue to the writer that the meaning in that section needs to be made clearer.

In Reports: Headings are used commonly in business writing because business people often need to locate specific information quickly without reading a whole document. Headings provide quick signals to the content of each section of a document. For example, notice how clearly the labels on the lab report below label the information in each section.

Product Reliability Test Report

Product Tested: _____

Date of Test: _____

Prepared by: _____

Manufacturer's Claim
Proctor & Gamble claims that Dawn Dishwashing Soap will "take grease out of your way."

Method of Testing
An average kitchen sink was filled with four gallons of hot water and two tablespoons of Dawn. A pan was generously coated with a layer of shortening (grease). The pan was then inserted into the water and washed clean. Following the pan, a dirty drinking glass was placed into the dishwater and washed clean. Both the pan and the glass came out of the water grease-free.

Conclusion
The test confirmed the claim. No greasy residue remained on either the pan or the glass. Proctor & Gamble's claim is accurate and valid.

One important rule in using headings—make them brief, clear, and directly related to content.

Notice that the headings **Manufacturer's Claim, Method of Testing,** and **Conclusion** clearly label the contents of each section. Study the headings and answer the questions below.

1) Where are the headings located on the page? _____
2) Are the headings in bold or regular type? _____
3) Are the headings larger than the other text? _____
4) Are the headings all caps or title case? _____
5) Are the headings single words or phrases? _____
6) Are the headings consistent in size and font? _____

Report Headings: Even though heading styles vary a lot, here are some standard guidelines to follow as you get started using headings to divide sections in your report writing.

1) Place section headlines flush left.
2) Make headlines bold.
3) Use 16 point font or larger.
4) Use all caps and underlines sparingly.
5) Keep headings brief and clear.
6) Make heading style consistent throughout a report.

Story Headings: Headings in stories are similar to headings in reports. However, different book publishers use different styles. In the model below, you will see headings from a table of contents and a story page. Notice that the publisher of this book has used a variety of headline styles—italics, bold, small caps, and four different sizes of lettering. However, also notice that all the headlines are in the same typeface (the same family of letter style). Consistency is important.

TABLE OF CONTENTS

Chapters

Chapter 4

Mingos in the Woods

Chingachgook held up the head of the fresh pipe he had found in the bushes. The bowl was soapstone and had been carved with great skill. In the center was a Catholic cross. This sign alerted the Pathfinder to the presence of Mingos, who were allies of the French.

"Has the enemy got between us and our port?" asked Cap.

The Pathfinder answered that there was an enemy war party downstream and that the group's safety depended on concealing its presence. At the same time, they needed to create a diversion that would draw the Mingos upstream past their group. Then they could

Study the pages above and then answer the following questions about the headlines used.

1. What headline is in 20-point font? _____

2. Which headline is in italics? _____

3. Which headline is in small caps? _____

4. Which headline is title case bold? _____

Making Choices

A. Headings in Reports

Use the report model in this chapter. Rewrite one of your recent classroom reports. Divide it into sections and give each section a heading, following the guidelines you have learned. Then prepare a table of contents and title page for your report.

B. Headings in Stories

Use the story model in this chapter. Retell one of your favorite books or stories in your own words. Write it for a younger audience (six- or seven-year-olds). As you write, divide the story into chapters and give each chapter a title. Make these chapter titles your headings. Then prepare a table of contents page and a title page for your story.

Providing Visual Information

Understanding Choices

Appearance Matters!

A reader responds to the look of the page before its content is ever considered. Visual information gets your readers' attention and gives them an impression of your writing before they ever begin to read. In fact, a reader may decide whether or not to read an article based on appearance and that first impression!

Just think about your own reading habits. The first things on a page that grab your attention are the pictures, then the headlines, and then any enlarged quotations or other graphics. After you have surveyed the page, you decide what you will read. Professional writers use this knowledge of readers' habits in preparing mockups (rough designs) of their own pages.

They also know that the reader's eye tends to follow a "Z" movement across the page, which means that the eye moves from the upper left of a page across to the upper right, then down to the lower left and then across to the lower right—that makes the four corners of a page the most "looked at" positions and, therefore, the places to put the most attention-getting elements. Look at today's newspaper and answer the following questions about the front page.

What gets your attention first? _____

_____

What gets your attention next? _____

_____

Are these graphic elements or text? _____

> **A reader responds to the look of the page before its content is ever considered. . .**

Recognizing Choices

Creating headlines: Newspaper editors know that headlines attract readers to articles and stories and provide important information up front. A headline must tie in closely to the main point of the article it introduces. Most headlines are combinations of primary headlines and secondary headlines. Here are a few of the traditional guidelines for creating good headlines.

1. Be specific—tell the reader something important (rather than just supplying a label).
2. Reflect the tone of the article—a humorous article should have a humorous headline.
3. Use descriptive nouns and strong verbs.
4. Write headlines in present tense.
5. Avoid beginning a headline with *a*, *an*, or *the*.
6. Avoid using the same words in the headline that you use for the first line of the story.
7. Make primary headlines shorter than secondary headlines.
8. Put primary headlines in a larger font.
9. Position primary headlines right above the story.
10. Position secondary headlines below, above, to the left, or to the right of the primary headline.

Look in magazines and newspapers for headlines that catch your attention. Try to find headlines that demonstrate the above guidelines.

1. _____

2. _____

3. _____

4. _____

5. _____

6. _____

7. _____

8. _____

9. _____

10. _____

Name _____

Headlines: Newspapers use many different types of headlines. There will always be a primary headline, and, often, there will be a secondary headline along with the primary headline. Four common types of secondary headlines are the *kicker,* the *hammer,* the *tripod,* and the *wicket.* Read the following descriptions of each type and then identify each sample headline below as one of these types.

• Kicker: a secondary headline above the primary headline

• Hammer: a secondary headline below the primary headline (also called a reverse kicker)

• Wicket: a secondary headline of several lines above or below the primary headline

• Tripod: a secondary headline of several lines to the right or left of the primary headline

<u>**Winter Headaches Back**</u>
SNOW HALTS TOURNEY

_____

More Games
Microsoft announces new interactive games

_____

Allentown Sharks Upset Rival
Panthers to Take First Place in
Last Meet of Swim Finals
SHS SWIMMERS TAKE HOME GOLD

_____

Infinite Possibilities | *No limits due to age, gender, or training requirements. Here are great job opportunities.*

_____

Educational toys growing in popularity

_____

FLORIDA FUN FARES
If you're feeling cold, fly south to the sun this winter on ATA's low fares.

_____

Now look in newspapers and magazines and locate one of each of these four types of headlines. Paste them below.

KICKER

HAMMER

WICKET

TRIPOD

*Answers to page 103: (left to right, top to bottom) kicker, hammer, wicket, tripod, kicker, wicket

Bullets: Besides headings and headlines, there are some other useful tools for providing visual information. These include columns, charts, graphs, and bullets. For example, a bulleted list of items (like the list below) is very "reader friendly." Instead of presenting the main points in a paragraph, the writer presents each main point in a list.

- graphs

- columns

- charts

- bullets

Read the paragraph below. Find five types of academic writing mentioned in the paragraph. List the five types of writing using bullets to provide quick visual information. Be creative—draw your own bullets. Try circles, diamonds, arrows, or even an object that represents the type of item you are listing.

> Most academic programs include instruction in many different types of writing. Students in the primary grades usually learn how to write short stories. In the middle grades, they begin to write different types of reports for language arts, social studies, and science classes. They may even compose business letters and personal letters. Then in high school, students learn to write research papers in required classes and often study creative writing in optional classes which help them compose their own drama and poetry.

Types of Academic Writing

The SHS Gazette

Headline

With a Rule Line and a Kicker

Now design your own one-page brochure or newsletter. First you will need to determine your layout, that is, what will go on your page and how those elements will be arranged. Your preliminary sketch of this page is called a *mockup.* In preparing a mockup, you must decide on the following

- Name of your publication
- Content of articles
- Headlines for articles
- Photographs, charts, pull quotes
- Rule lines, bullets, white space

Another important characteristic of most newspapers and brochures is the arrangement of information in columns. Editors must decide how many columns they want on their pages, and they must also decide what kind of margin edges they will use for their columns.

Notice that, on this page, the columns are justified (even) on both the left and the right sides, leaving no ragged (uneven) margin on either side. Newspapers and brochures usually use justified edges to give a neat appearance to their columns. However, justified margins, as you can see from this page, cause irregular spaces in the middle of the lines. For this reason, justified margins are not used in reports and letters, where irregular spacing in lines that extend all the way across the page would be distracting for the reader.

You may also want to include a *pull quote,* which is a common graphic used in brochures and newsletters. The pull quote

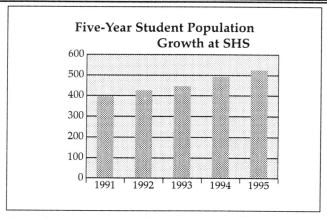

Five-Year Student Population Growth at SHS

is a line or two from an article in your brochure, which is enlarged and enclosed in a box to draw attention to a main idea in the article. Remember that white space also attracts readers' attention. Notice how the white space in the box helps draw attention to the content of the pull quote below.

> *The pull quote draws attention to a main idea in the article.*

Describe the content of your brochure.

_____

Give it a name. _____

How many columns?_____

What pictures? _____

_____

What graphics? _____

_____

What headlines?_____

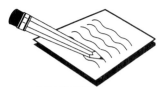

CHAPTER 6
Using Punctuation for Effect

Using Commas for Clarity and Emphasis

Understanding Choices

Although much of the punctuation that you use in your writing is dictated by rules—or "conventions"—of writing, you also have considerable freedom to choose when to use marks of punctuation and what marks to use. Your choices reflect both the effect that you wish to create and your personal style. In the work of professional writers, you see a wide range of punctuation practices. For example, many writers like the flair and vitality of the dash, whereas other writers rarely use it. Similarly, some writers use a lot of commas and others very few. Regardless of personal styles, however, the guiding principle is how best to convey the intended meaning.

Originally conceived as "breathing marks" for reading out loud, commas still serve to let the reader take a breath. Although too many commas in a sentence can slow the pace, too few can create confusion. Commas are generally used in the following situations:

- introductory words, phrases, and clauses
- compound sentences
- interrupting words, phrases, and clauses
- items in a series
- whenever misunderstanding would otherwise occur

Sometimes you can choose whether to use a comma or not. Following are some guidelines for using commas to create clarity and emphasis.

Introductory Words, Phrases, and Clauses
Commas are customarily used after long introductory elements. On the lines below, write a similar sentence of your own.

> When Lois bought her horse Silver Shetan, she had a difficult time loading him into the horse trailer.

When _____

_____

Using commas after shorter phrases or using too many commas can result in choppiness and detract from what you want to say. It is often better to rewrite a sentence to avoid unnecessary commas. The first sentence below is too choppy. The second is much easier to read. In the lines below, write similar sentences of your own.

> After a short run, Silver Shetan, Lois's new gelding, decided that he wanted to go back to the barn for supper.

After _____, _____, _____, _____

_____.

> After a short run Lois's new gelding Silver Shetan decided that he wanted to go back to the barn for supper.

After _____

_____.

Sometimes the comma is necessary for clarity. The sentence below misleads readers. They think they are getting advice on how to improve study habits. Supply the necessary comma. Then, on the line below, write a similar sentence of your own.

> If you want to improve your study habits must change.

If _____, _____.

Commas are used after words such as *however, consequently, furthermore,* and *obviously.* They are not usually used after the words *and, nor, but, for, or,* and *yet.* In the following pairs of sentences, notice that the comma after *however* creates emphasis by slowing down the reading. It also creates a more formal tone. Both pairs of sentences are correct: the better choice is the one that creates the desired effect. Create similar sentences of your own.

The puppy was difficult to train. Yet no one would want to give her up.
The puppy was difficult to train. However, no one would want to give her up.

The _____. Yet _____

_____.

The _____. However, _____

_____.

Name _____

Compound Sentences
Compound sentences usually require commas before the coordinating conjunction. In the sentence below, provide the necessary comma.

> Gary loved cooking exotic dishes for his mother and Karla did nothing to discourage his interest.

In some short compound sentences, the commas can be omitted. Notice that a comma is not needed for clarity in either of the sentences below. In fact, using a comma changes the meaning a little. By slowing down the reading, the comma emphasizes the second half of the sentence. Write your own sentence following each pattern.

Brian bought the book but Anne read it.   Brian bought the book, but Anne read it.

_____   _____,

but _____ .   but _____ .

Interrupting Words, Phrases, and Clauses
Interrupting elements that add helpful, but not essential, information are often set off by commas. Choose one of these patterns to imitate.

> Jennifer, incidentally, has won another award for soccer.
> It was Jennifer, not Shawn, who made the winning goal.

_____, _____, _____ .

In other cases, whether you use the comma or not changes the meaning entirely. Look at the two sentences below and place a check mark on the appropriate line.

> Americans who eat a lot of red meat are increasingly at risk for heart disease.

Who is at risk? All Americans _____ Only those who eat a lot of red meat _____

> Americans, who eat a lot of red meat, are increasingly at risk for heart disease.

Who is at risk? All Americans _____ Only those who eat a lot of red meat _____

Below create similar sentences of your own, one with commas and one without.

Teenagers _____

Teenagers _____

*Answer, page 108: If you want to improve, your study habits must change.

Items in a Series

Commas usually separate words, phrases, or clauses in a series. Whether you use the comma before *and* is a matter of personal preference, but you should be consistent. Because it is never wrong to use the comma before *and*, it may be safer simply to use it. Below insert the commas to make it clear that *cheese and crackers* and *stocks and bonds* are all separate items.

At the convenience store I bought bread, milk, cheese and crackers.
Ernie trades in commodities, stocks and bonds.

Write a sentence using a series.

_____   _____and _____.

Commas sometimes separate adjectives, but not always. If both of the adjectives modify the noun equally, commas are needed. Otherwise they are not. In the first sentence below both *bright* and *feathery-tailed* describe the *Hale-Bopp comet*. In the second sentence *bright* says more about the intensity of *white* than about *Hale-Bopp*. Thus, the comma is unnecessary. On the lines below, write sentences following each pattern.

The bright, feathery-tailed Hale-Bopp comet is a magnificent picture in the night sky. The bright white Hale-Bopp comet created a magnificent picture in the night sky.

The _____, _____ _____.
The _____.

Whenever Misunderstanding Would Otherwise Occur

Often commas are needed simply to prevent confusion. See whether you can figure out where the commas belong in the following four sentences.

a) In the world of television appearances mean everything.

b) In the world of television appearances style means everything.

c) In most cases we have seen improvement in test scores begins following treatment.

d) In most cases we have seen improvement in test scores following treatment.

*Answer, page 109: Gary loved cooking exotic dishes for his mother, and Karla did nothing to discourage his interest.

Recognizing Choices

The following sentences from the introduction to *Arabian Nights* have had seven commas removed. Put them where you think they belong.

People in different countries tell them differently but they are always the same stories really whether among little Zulus at the Cape or little Eskimo near the North Pole. The changes are only in matters of manners and customs such as wearing clothes or not meeting lions who talk in the warm countries or talking to bears in the cold countries. There are plenty of kings and queens in the fairy tales just because long ago there were plenty of kings in the country.

Here is how the passage reads with the commas replaced.

People in different countries tell them differently, (1) but they are always the same stories, (2) really, (3) whether among little Zulus at the Cape or little Eskimo near the North Pole. The changes are only in matters of manners and customs, (4) such as wearing clothes or not, (5) meeting lions who talk in the warm countries, (6) or talking to bears in the cold countries. There are plenty of kings and queens in the fairy tales, (7) just because long ago there were plenty of kings in the country.

Each of the commas above is numbered. In the spaces below tell why the comma is used, using one of these reasons:

        a) introductory words, phrases, and clauses
        b) interrupting words, phrases, and clauses
        c) compound sentences
        d) items in a series
        e) whenever misunderstanding would otherwise occur

1._____   2. _____   3._____

4._____   5. _____   6._____

7._____

*Answers, page 110: At the convenience store I bought bread, milk, cheese, and crackers. Ernie trades in commodities, stocks, and bonds. In the world of television, appearances mean everything. In the world of television appearances, style means everything. In most cases we have seen, improvement in test scores begins following treatment. In most cases, we have seen improvement in test scores following treatment.

Making Choices

Think of all the careers that you have ever wanted to have, starting with your earliest memories. In a short essay below, explain what the careers were and your reasons for wanting them. Include in your essay at least one comma for each of the uses in the list below. Number the commas in your essay, and list the numbers in the appropriate spaces below.

Careers I Have Imagined

_____

_____

_____

_____

_____

_____

_____

_____

_____

_____

_____

_____

_____

_____

_____   introductory words, phrases, and clauses

_____   interrupting words, phrases, and clauses

_____   compound sentences

_____   items in a series

_____   whenever misunderstanding would otherwise occur

*Answers, page 111: 1. c, 2. b, 3. b, 4. b or e, 5. d, 6. d, 7. b or e

© Instructional Fair • TS Denison   112   IF2536 Beyond the Rules

Choosing Among Periods, Semicolons, and Commas

Understanding Choices

Although some rules for periods, semicolons, and commas are quite distinct, occasionally they are interchangeable, depending on the effect you want to create.

Periods, Semicolons, and Commas

To avoid a series of choppy sentences and to create sentence variety, you can combine two sentences with a semicolon. Sentences joined this way need to be closely linked in meaning. On the lines below, create similar sentences of your own.

Mike's two sisters love to spend time with him. Both find him greatly entertaining.
Mike's two sisters love to spend time with him; both find him greatly entertaining.

1. _____

   _____

2. _____

   _____

A third way to connect sentences is to use conjunctions to separate the items. Notice in the second pair of sentences below that the conjunction serves the reader in two ways: (1) it eliminates the choppiness, and (2) it alerts the reader that the second part of the sentence will show contrast. Create similar sentences of your own.

Mocha and Dino are dogs. They live better than many people.
Mocha and Dino are dogs, but they live better than many people.

1. _____ and _____ are _____. They _____

   _____ .

2. _____ and _____ are_____, but they _____

   _____ .

Semicolons and Commas

Although commas usually separate items in a series, readers can get confused if commas are also used within the series. To solve this problem, thoughtful writers often use semicolons to separate the items. The first sentence below is difficult to read because of all the commas. Circle two places where semicolons could replace commas to make the series easier to read.

Twenty years ago few schools imagined that before long they would be using networked writing labs, where students would be reading one another's papers on screen, high-tech graphics software, which would enable students to do desk-top publishing, and Internet hookups, which would put students in touch with people around the world.

As with items in a series, independent clauses that have internal punctuation are easier to read if they are separated with semicolons, even if they are joined by a conjunction. Circle the comma that could be replaced by a semicolon to make the sentence clearer.

Twenty years ago, when computers were used almost exclusively by businesses, schools relied on pen and paper—and an occasional typewriter—to communicate, but many schools now use networked writing labs, e-mail, and Internet hookups, enabling students to "reach out" to the world.

Commas and Conjunctions

For emphasis with coordinate elements, try using a comma rather than *and*. The first sentence below has a compound direct object: *to fight fires* and *to ride in big red trucks and save lives.* The second sentence replaces the *and* with a comma, making the sentence clearer and more pleasing to the ear.

As a child I always wanted to fight fires *and* to ride in big red trucks and save lives.
As a child I always wanted to fight fires, to ride in big red trucks and save lives.

As a child I always wanted to _____

and to _____ .

As a child I always wanted to _____ ,

to _____ .

Recognizing Choices

The following sentences from *Anne of Green Gables* by Lucy Maud Montgomery have had two semicolons removed. Put them where you think they belong.

Marilla was a tall, thin woman, with angles and without curves her dark hair showed some gray streaks and was always twisted up in a hard little knot behind with two wire hairpins stuck aggressively through it. She looked like a woman of narrow experience and rigid conscience, which she was but there was a saving something about her mouth which, if it had been ever so slightly developed, might have been considered indicative of a sense of humor.

Here is how the passage reads with the semicolons supplied.

Marilla was a tall, thin woman, with angles and without curves; (1) her dark hair showed some gray streaks and was always twisted up in a hard little knot behind with two wire hairpins stuck aggressively through it. She looked like a woman of narrow experience and rigid conscience, which she was; (2) but there was a saving something about her mouth which, if it had been ever so slightly developed, might have been considered indicative of a sense of humor.

Each of the semicolons above is numbered. In the spaces below tell why the semicolon is used.

     a) to combine two sentences
     b) to separate independent clauses that have internal commas

1. _____   2. _____

*Answers, page 114: Twenty years ago few schools imagined that before long they would be using networked writing labs, where students would be reading one another's papers on screen; high-tech graphics software, which would enable students to do desk-top publishing; and Internet hookups, which would put students in touch with people around the world. Twenty years ago, when computers were used almost exclusively by businesses, schools relied on pen and paper—and an occasional typewriter—to communicate; but many schools now use networked writing labs, e-mail, and Internet hookups, enabling students to "reach out" to the world.

Making Choices

Think of a family legend that you have heard over and over in your family from a parent, grandparent, or some other relative. Maybe the legend is about something the relative did when a child, something the family did—some difficulty they endured or some honor they earned—or some interesting job. Include in your essay each of the comma and semicolon patterns listed below. Number the sentences in your essay, and put the numbers in the appropriate spaces below.

Family Legend

_____

_____

_____

_____

_____

_____

_____

_____

_____

_____

_____

_____

_____

_____ combine two sentences with a semicolon

_____ combine two sentences with a comma and a conjunction

_____ use semicolons to separate independent clauses with internal commas

_____ use a comma rather than *and* with coordinate elements

*Answers, page 115: 1. a, 2. b

Choosing Among Dashes, Parentheses, Commas, and Colons

Understanding Choices

Although you do not have a lot of choice about some punctuation rules, you have a great deal of choice about others, depending on the effect you want to create and your relationship with the reader. Look at these three sentences.

a) Karla, whom I trust, has told me the most incredible story.
b) Karla (whom I trust) has told me the most incredible story.
c) Karla—whom I trust—has told me the most incredible story.

Which seems most lively? _____
Which appears to be more formal? _____
Which appears as though you were almost whispering the information? _____

You probably thought "c" was most lively, "a" most formal, and "b" like a whispered comment.

Parentheses or Dashes?

When inserting informational comments into a sentence, parentheses give the impression that the information is confidential. It is a good choice for explanatory information. A dash, on the other hand, is not at all secretive. It is casual, lively, and abrupt, almost as though the writer had just thought of the comment. As a writer you need to decide which of these reactions you want from your reader. One of the following sentences from Mark Twain's *Tom Sawyer* uses the dash to set off the italicized material, and the other sentence uses parentheses. See whether you can guess which marks of punctuation Twain used in each situation. Supply the punctuation. (Remember, either would be grammatically correct. You are guessing Twain's preference. Twain's choice is given on the following page.)

Tom's younger brother *or rather half-brother* Sid was already through with his part of the work *picking up chips* for he was a quiet boy and had no adventurous, troublesome ways.

While Tom was eating his supper, and stealing sugar as opportunity offered, Aunt Polly asked him questions that were full of guile, and very deep *for she wanted to trap him into damaging revealments.*

Commas or Dashes?

Dashes can be especially helpful when a sentence has commas separating items in a series. Compare the reading difficulty in the two sentences below.

Students who take the full load of academic subjects, English, mathematics, science, social studies, and a foreign language, become very efficient in using their time, mostly because they find they have so little of it.

Students who take the full load of academic subjects—English, mathematics, science, social studies, and a foreign language—become very efficient in using their time, mostly because they find they have so little of it.

Complete the sentence below by supplying the names of educational TV channels or programs.

Preschool children who watch major educational television programs—_____

_____—learn important reading strategies.

Dashes or Colons?

When you want to prepare the reader for a list, example, or summary, you can choose between a dash or a colon. If you want to be more formal, you would choose a colon. If you want to appear more spontaneous, you would choose a dash. Both marks of punctuation are ways of saying, "Here comes the information" or "Here comes the point." In the following sentences from Stephen Crane's *The Red Badge of Courage,* see whether you can guess which sentence used a dash and which used a colon. Supply the punctuation.

Later, he had gone down to his mother's room and had spoken thus "Ma, I'm going to enlist."

"You watch out, Henry, an' take good care of yerself in this here fighting business you watch, an' take good care of yerself."

Often dashes or colons are helpful between a subject list (*Math, English, science* in the sentences below) and a word or phrase that summarizes that list (*these subjects).* Write your own sentences about movies, music, or sports below, one using a colon and one using dashes.

Math, English, and science—these subjects are emphasized in all standardized tests.
Math, English, and science: these subjects are emphasized in all standardized tests.

_____

_____

*Answers, page 117: Tom's younger brother (or rather half-brother) Sid was already through with his part of the work (picking up chips) for he was a quiet boy and had no adventurous, troublesome ways. While Tom was eating his supper, and stealing sugar as opportunity offered, Aunt Polly asked him questions that were full of guile, and very deep—for she wanted to trap him into damaging revealments.

Recognizing Choices

Decide what punctuation you would use for each of the following sentences: dashes, parentheses, commas, or colons. Insert the punctuation that you prefer. In the blank, indicate which choices would be available to you in each sentence, using one of the following combinations.

         a) dash or colon
         b) dash or parentheses
         c) comma, dash, or parentheses

_____ 1. After the date Deborah was certain of one thing she would not be seeing Bill again.

_____ 2. All his friends thought that the breakup was too soon all her friends thought that it wasn't soon enough.

_____ 3. Friends even ones she hardly knew called to congratulate her.

_____ 4. Deborah found great pleasure in her new independence she renewed old friendships, made new ones, and spent more time with her beloved dogs Dino and Mocha.

Lewis Carroll's *Alice's Adventures in Wonderland* makes frequent use of parentheses. Read the following passages containing three sets of parentheses.

    She generally gave herself very good advice **(though she very seldom followed it)**, and sometimes she scolded herself so severely as to bring tears to her eyes. . . .
    There seemed to be no use in waiting by the little door, so she went back to the table, half hoping she might find another key on it, or at any rate a book of rules for shutting people up like telescopes: this time she found a little bottle on it **("which certainly was not here before," said Alice)**, and round the neck of the bottle was a paper label, with the words "DRINK ME" beautifully printed on it in large letters. . . .
    However, this bottle was NOT marked "poison," so Alice ventured to taste it, and finding it very nice **(it had, in fact, a sort of mixed flavour of sherry-tart, custard, pineapple, roast turkey, toffee, and hot buttered toast)**, she very soon finished it off.
    "What a curious feeling!" said Alice; "I must be shutting up like a telescope."
    And so it was indeed: she was now only ten inches high, and her face brightened up at the thought that she was now the right size for going through the little door into that lovely garden.

On the lines below write several sentences telling what Alice found in the garden. Use at least one set of parentheses in your part of the story.

_____

_____

_____

*Answers, page 118: Later, he had gone down to his mother's room and had spoken thus: "Ma, I'm going to enlist." "You watch out, Henry, an' take good care of yerself in this here fighting business—you watch, an' take good care of yerself."

Making Choices

A Ghost Story

Read the following passage from Mark Twain's "A Ghost Story," which includes frequent use of the dash. On the lines below write a conclusion for the story, maintaining the ideas, sentence patterns, and tone of the original. Use dashes, parentheses, and colons at least once.

I slept profoundly, but how long I do not know. All at once I found myself awake, and filled with a shuddering expectancy. All was still. All but my own heart—I could hear it beat. Presently the bedclothes began to slip away slowly toward the foot of the bed, as if someone were pulling them! I could not stir; I could not speak. . . . At last I roused my energies and snatched the covers back to their place and held them with a strong grip. I waited. By and by I felt a faint tug, and took a fresh grip. The tug strengthened to a steady strain—it grew stronger and stronger. My hold parted, and for the third time the blankets slid away. I groaned. An answering groan came from the foot of the bed! Beaded drops of sweat stood upon my forehead. I was more dead than alive. Presently I heard a heavy footstep in my room—the step of an elephant, it seemed to me it was not like anything human. But it was moving FROM me—there was relief in that. I heard it approach the door—pass out without moving bolt or lock—and wander away among the dismal corridors, straining the floors and joists till they creaked again as it passed—and then silence reigned once more.

_____

_____

_____

_____

_____

_____

_____

_____

_____

_____

_____

_____

Compare your story with those of your classmates.

Using Hyphens in Compound Words

Understanding Choices

Words are hyphenated when they are so closely connected in meaning that they almost seem to be one word. Many compound words start out as two words, gradually becoming hyphenated, and eventually becoming a single word (*note + book = notebook, grand + mother = grandmother*). A modern, very rapid version of this process is seen in the term electronic mail, which quickly became *e-mail* to most users and is now frequently written *email*. The process of going from two words to one word usually takes much longer, though, so it is important to consult a dictionary to be certain whether a word is hyphenated or not. If a compound word is not found in the dictionary, it probably should be written as two words.

Compound Modifiers

Writers often hyphenate compound adjectives that come before a noun to help the reader avoid confusion. One of the following sentences needs a hyphen and the other a comma. Make the sentences easier for the reader by supplying the appropriate punctuation.

The ice covered roads making driving treacherous.
The ice covered roads made driving treacherous.

Normally writers use the hyphen only when the adjectives come before the noun, not after, because there is much less chance of confusion when the adjective follows the noun. Notice below that hyphenating "ice-covered" would not make it any clearer.

Driving is treacherous when roads are <u>ice covered</u>.

Similarly, hyphens are not used with adverbs that end in "ly" or with the words *most* and *more*.

<u>Heavily iced</u> roads make driving treacherous.
The <u>most treacherous</u> roads are those with ice and heavy traffic.

Specially Coined Compounds

Sometimes writers create their own compounds—or coinages—to make ideas more descriptive. These coinages, which can be either adjectives or nouns, are always hyphenated.

Jenny is a real major-leaguer.
I gave the gate-crasher a why-don't-you-just-get-lost look.

Recognizing Choices

Following are two passages in which authors use hyphenated words to make their writing more interesting. The first is a passage from Rudyard Kipling's *The Jungle Book*, which includes five noun coinages. On the lines below, rewrite each phrase or clause to avoid the coinage. Read the revised passage aloud and discuss the effect of the hyphenated compound words.

It was the jackal—Tabaqui, the **Dish-licker.** The wolves of India despise Tabaqui because he runs about making mischief, telling tales, and eating rags and pieces of leather from the village **rubbish-heaps**. . . . The Law of the Jungle . . . forbids every beast to eat Man except when he is killing to show his children how to kill, and then he must hunt outside the **hunting-grounds** of his pack or tribe. The real reason for this is that **man-killing** means, sooner or later, the arrival of white men on elephants, with guns. . . . Then everybody in the jungle suffers. The reason the beasts give among themselves is that Man is the weakest and most defenseless of all living things, and it is unsportsmanlike to touch him. They say too—and it is true—that **man-eaters** become mangy, and lose their teeth.

Coinage	Rewritten
Dish-licker	jackal who licks dishes
rubbish-heaps	_____
hunting-grounds	_____
man-killing	_____
man-eaters	_____

Rewrite the adjective coinages in the following passage from Jack London's "To Build a Fire."

North and south, as far as his eye could see, it was unbroken white, save for a dark hairline that curved and twisted from around the **spruce-covered** island to the south, and that curved and twisted away into the north, where it disappeared behind another **spruce-covered** island. . . . But all this—the mysterious, **far-reaching** hairline trail, the absence of sun from the sky, the tremendous cold, and the strangeness and weirdness of it all—made no impression on the man. . . . He was a **warm-whiskered** man, but the hair on his face did not protect the high cheekbones and the eager nose that thrust itself aggressively into the frosty air. At the man's heels trotted a dog, a big native husky, the proper wolf dog, **gray-coated** and without any visible or temperamental difference from its brother, the wild wolf.

Coinage	Rewritten
spruce-covered	island covered with spruce trees
far-reaching	_____
warm-whiskered	_____
gray-coated	_____

Jack London uses hyphenated words frequently in *The Call of the Wild*. Sometimes the hyphenated words are compound adjectives, and sometimes they are nouns. In the blanks below (1) write the hyphenated word and (2) tell whether it is an adjective or noun.

Hyphenated Word   **Noun or Adjective**

_____ _____ 1. Buck lived at a big house in the sun-kissed Santa Clara Valley.

_____ _____ 2. The house was approached by graveled driveways which wound about through wide-spreading lawns and under the interlacing boughs of tall poplars.

_____ _____ 3. Then the rope was removed, and he was flung into a cage-like crate.

_____ _____ 4. But the saloon-keeper let him alone, and in the morning four men entered and picked up the crate.

_____ _____ 5. More tormentors Buck decided, for they were evil-looking creatures, ragged and unkempt; and he stormed and raged at them through the bars.

_____ _____ 6. He did not mind the hunger so much, but the lack of water caused him severe suffering and fanned his wrath to a fever-pitch.

_____ _____ 7. Four men gingerly carried the crate from the wagon to a small, high-walled back yard.

_____ _____ 8. "Now, you red-eyed devil," he said when he had made an opening sufficient for the passage of Buck's body.

_____ _____ 9. In mid-air, just as his jaws were about to close on the man, he received a shock that checked his body and brought his teeth together with an agonizing clip.

_____ _____ 10. With a roar that was almost lion-like in its ferocity, he again hurled himself at the man.

Making Choices

The following poem by Robert Louis Stevenson tells of a children's game. It also includes several hyphenated words. Write your own poem or short story describing some game you played as a child. Include hyphenated words used both as nouns and as adjectives. Underline your coinages.

A Good Play

We built a ship upon the stairs
All made of the back-bedroom chairs,
And filled it full of soft pillows
To go a-sailing on the billows.

We took a saw and several nails,
And water in the nursery pails;
And Tom said, "Let us also take
An apple and a slice of cake;"—
Which was enough for Tom and me
To go a-sailing on, till tea.

We sailed along for days and days,
And had the very best of plays;
But Tom fell out and hurt his knee,
So there was no one left but me.

_____

_____

_____

_____

_____

_____

_____

_____

_____

_____

Read your poem or story to your classmates.

*Answers, page 124: 1. adj., 2. adj., 3. adj., 4. n., 5. adj., 6. n., 7. adj., 8. adj., 9. n., 10. adj.